THE POLYSYLLABIC SPREE

THE
POLYSYLLABIC
SPREE

BY
NICK HORNBY

BELIEVER BOOKS

a division of
MᶜSWEENEY'S

BELIEVER BOOKS
a division of
McSWEENEY'S

826 Valencia Street
San Francisco, CA 94110

These pieces appeared between September 2003
and November 2004 in the *Believer* magazine.
Additional copyright information appears on page 145.

www.believermag.com

Cover design by Sam Potts.

Printed in Canada by Westcan Printing Group.

ISBN: 1-932416-24-2

ALSO BY THE AUTHOR

Fever Pitch
High Fidelity
About a Boy
Speaking with the Angel (editor)
How to Be Good
Songbook

To Dave and Vendela

TABLE OF CONTENTS

SEPTEMBER 2003

BOOKS BOUGHT:
* *Robert Lowell: A Biography*—Ian Hamilton
* *Collected Poems*—Robert Lowell
* *Against Oblivion: Some of the Lives of the 20th-Century Poets*—Ian Hamilton
* *In Search of J. D. Salinger*—Ian Hamilton
* *Nine Stories*—J. D. Salinger
* *Franny and Zooey*—J. D. Salinger
* *Raise High the Roof Beam, Carpenters/Seymour: An Introduction*—J. D. Salinger
* *The Ern Malley Affair*—Michael Heyward
* *Something Happened*—Joseph Heller
* *Penguin Modern Poets 5*—Corso/Ferlinghetti/Ginsberg

BOOKS READ:
* All the Salinger
* *In Search of Salinger* and *Lowell*
* Some of *Against Oblivion*
* *Pompeii* by Robert Harris (not bought)

So this is supposed to be about the how, and when, and why, and what of reading—about the way that, when reading is going well, one book leads to another and to another, a paper trail of theme and meaning; and how, when it's going badly, when books don't stick or take, when your mood and the mood of the book are fighting like cats, you'd rather do anything but attempt the next paragraph, or reread the last one for the tenth time. "We talked about books," says a character in Charles Baxter's wonderful *Feast of Love*, "how boring they were to read,

13

but how you loved them anyway." Anyone who hasn't felt like that isn't owning up.

But first, some ground rules:

1) I don't want anyone writing in to point out that I spend too much money on books, many of which I will never read. I know that already. I certainly *intend* to read all of them, more or less. My *intentions* are good. Anyway, it's my money. And I'll bet you do it too.

2) Similarly, I don't want anyone pointing out that certain books I write about in this column are by friends—or, in the case of *Pompeii,* by brothers-in-law. A lot of my friends are writers, and so some of my reading time is, inevitably, spent on their books. I won't attempt to disguise the connections, if that makes anyone feel better. Anyway, it's been five years since my brother-in-law, the author of *Fatherland* and *Enigma,* produced a book, so the chances are that I'll have been fired from the *Believer* before he comes up with another one. (I may have been fired even before *this* one is published, in September.)

3) And don't waste your breath trying to tell me that I'm showing off. This month, maybe, I'm showing off a little. (Or am I? Shouldn't I have read some of these books decades ago? *Franny and Zooey*? Jesus. Maybe I'm doing the opposite: maybe I'm humiliating myself. And maybe you have read all these *and loads of others,* in the last fortnight. I don't know you. What's—ahem—a normal amount, for someone with a job and kids, who watches TV?) But next month I may spend my allotted space desperately trying to explain how come I've only managed three pages of a graphic novel and the sports

section of the *Daily Mirror* in four whole weeks—in which case, please don't bother accusing me of philistinism, laziness, or pig-ignorance. I read a lot this month (*a*) because it's the summer, and it's been hot, and I haven't been working very hard, and there's no football on TV and (*b*) because my eldest son, for reasons we don't need to go into, has spent even more time than usual stuck in the toilet, and I have to sit outside on a chair. Thus do books get read.

This month, it went something like:

Against Oblivion →
Lowell → *In Search of Salinger* → *Nine Stories* → *Raise High the Roof Beam, Carpenters* → *(Pompeii)* → *Seymour: An Introduction* → *Franny and Zooey*

The Robert Lowell–Ian Hamilton thing began with Anthony Lane's intimidatingly brilliant review of Lowell's collected poems in the *New Yorker*: Lane mentioned in passing that Hamilton's biography was still the best available. Even so, I wouldn't have bothered if it hadn't been for several other factors, the most important of which is that my baby son is called Lowell. We named him thus partly after various musicians—Lowell George and the blues singer Lowell Fulson—and partly because of Robert Lowell, whose work we had never read (in our defense, he is no longer terribly well-known here in England, and he isn't taught in school), but whose existence persuaded us, in our untrustworthy hormonal state, that the name had a generic artistic connotation. Our Lowell will almost certainly turn out to be a sales manager for a sportswear firm, whose only contact with literature is when he listens to Tom Clancy audiobooks once a year on holiday—not that there's anything wrong with that.

On top of that, I had recently watched a BBC documentary about Ian Hamilton himself, who was a good poet and a great critic, and a mentor to Barnes, Amis, McEwan, and that whole generation of English writers. (There is, by the way, an exceptionally good new BBC cable channel here, BBC4, which shows documentaries of similar merit and obscurity every night of the week.) And I'd met him a couple of times, and really liked him, not least because he wrote an enthusiastic review of my first book. (Did I mention that he was a great critic?) He died a couple of years ago, and I wish I'd known him better.

I still wouldn't necessarily have tracked down the Lowell biography, however, if I hadn't spent a weekend near Hay-on-Wye. Hay is a weird town on the border of England and Wales that consists almost entirely of secondhand bookshops—there are forty of 'em within a few hundred yards of each other—and one of which is an immaculately stocked poetry store. That's where I found Hamilton's book, as well as the Penguin Modern Poets collection, purchased because Corso's lovely "Marriage" was read at a friend's wedding recently. I bought the Ern Malley book (for a pound, pure maybe-one-day whimsy, doomed to top-shelf oblivion), and a first edition of *Something Happened* (because it crops up in *Stone Reader*), elsewhere in the town. Buying books is what you do in Hay, in the absence of any other options.

Despite all these various auguries, I hadn't necessarily expected to read every word of the Lowell biography, but Hamilton is such a good writer, and Lowell's life was so tumultuous, that it was gone in a couple of days, like an Elmore Leonard novel. Sometimes, in the hands of the right person, biographies of relatively minor figures (and Lowell's influence seems to be receding fast) are especially compelling: They seem to have their times and cultural environments written through them like a stick of rock, in a way that sui generis major figures sometimes don't. Lowell, it turns out, is the guy you can see just behind Zelig's shoulder: He corresponded with Eliot, hung out with Jackie and Bobby K., and traveled around with Eugene McCarthy in '68. He also beat up his own father, had endless strange, possibly sexless extramarital affairs with innumerable young women, and endured terrible periods of psychosis, frequently accompanied by alarming rants about Hitler. In other words, it's one of those books you thrust on your partner with an incredulous cry of "This is *me!*"

And as a bonus, I felt I learned more about the act of creating poetry from this one book than I did in my entire educational career. (A line from a letter Lowell wrote to Randall Jarrell that I shall endeavor to remember: "In prose you have to be interested in *what* is being said… it's very exciting for me, like going fishing.") In the end, the psychotic periods make for a wearying rhythm to the book, and perhaps Hamilton's criticism of the poems tends to be a little too astringent—the *Collected Poems* runs to twelve hundred pages, but Hamilton seems to argue that we could live without a good eleven hundred and fifty of them. And this is a poet he clearly loves…

But it's a great biography, and now I was off on this Hamilton kick. I bought *Against Oblivion,* his book of little essays about every major twentieth-century poet bar four—Eliot, Auden, Hardy, and Yeats—absent because their work is, in the critic's view, certain to survive; it's in the bathroom, and I've got through half of it. (Shock news: Grown-up critics think E. E. Cummings sucks. I honestly didn't know. I read him at school, put him in the "good" box, and left him there.) I vaguely remembered the story of Hamilton's attempt to write a biography of Salinger: it ended up in court, and Salinger actually broke cover to give a deposition to Hamilton's lawyer. Hamilton admits that Salinger's victory left gaping holes in the book he wanted to write. He was denied permission to quote from letters that are freely available for inspection in various libraries. I'm still glad I read it, though. I learned things—that you could earn $2,000 for a short story in the 1930s, for example. The stories about Salinger hustling for work, and dining gaily with the Oliviers in London, make one feel almost giddy,

17

so unlikely do they sound now; and when the Hamilton mind goes to work on the stories, it's something to see.

The realization that you could polish off a major author's entire oeuvre in less than a week was definitely part of the appeal—you won't catch Dickens being pushed around like that— but it was still tougher work than I thought it would be. Just about every one of *Nine Stories* is perfect, and *Raise High the Roof Beam, Carpenters* is fresh and funny, but *Seymour: An Introduction…* Man, I really didn't want to know about Seymour's ears. Or his eyes. Or whether he could play sports. The very first time I met him he blew his brains out (in "A Perfect Day for Bananafish"), so to be brutal, I never really developed as much curiosity about him as Salinger seems to want of me. But whereas I was expecting something light and sweet, I ended up with this queasy sense of the psychodramatic: I knew that I wouldn't be able to separate the stories from the Story, but I hadn't expected the author to collude in the confusion. Hamilton is especially good on how Buddy Glass, apparently Salinger's mouthpiece, creates and perpetuates myths about his alter ego.

I read *Pompeii* in between *Nine Stories* and *Raise High the Roof Beam…* It has to be a rule, I think, that when a family member gives you his new book, you stop what you're doing and read it. Having a brother-in-law for a writer could have turned out really, really badly. He could have been more or less successful than me. Or he could have written books that I hated, or found impossible to get through. (Imagine if your brother-in-law wrote *Finnegans Wake,* and you were really busy at work. Or you weren't really a big reader.) Luckily, his books are great, and a pleasure to read, and despite my trepidation—I couldn't see how he was going to pull off a thriller that ends with the biggest deus ex machina the world has ever known—this is, I reckon, his best one. Oh, and he read just about every book there is on volcanology and Roman water systems, as well as every word Pliny wrote, so my admiration for my sister has increased even further. Has she been sitting there listening to stuff about Roman water systems for the last three years? I now understand why her favorite film of recent years is *Legally Blonde*. How could it not be?

I read 55 percent of the books I bought this month—five and a half out of ten. Two of the unread books, however, are volumes of poetry, and, to my way of thinking, poetry books work more like books of reference: They go up on the shelves straight away (as opposed to onto the bedside table), to be taken down and dipped into every now and again. (And, before any outraged poets explode, I'd like to point out that I'm one of the seventy-three people in the world who buys poetry.) And anyway, anyone who is even contemplating ploughing straight through over a thousand pages of Lowell's poetry clearly needs a cable TV subscription, or maybe even some friends, a relationship, and a job. So if it's OK with you, I'm taking the poetry out, and calling it five and a half out of eight—and the Heller I've read before, years ago, so that's six and a half out of eight. I make that 81 $1/4$ percent! I am both erudite and financially prudent! I admit it: I haven't read a book about an Australian literary hoax (which, I repeat, I bought for a quid), and a handful of essays about people like James Wright, Robinson Jeffers, and Norman Cameron. Maybe there are slumbering pockets of ignorance best left undisturbed; no one likes a know-it-all. ✶

OCTOBER 2003

If you write books—or a certain kind of book, anyway—you can't resist a scan round the hotel swimming pool when you go on holiday. You just can't help yourself, despite the odds: you need to know, straight off, whether anyone is reading one of yours. You imagine spending your days under a parasol watching, transfixed and humbled, as a beautiful and intelligent young man or woman, almost certainly a future best friend, maybe even spouse, weeps and guffaws through three hundred pages of your brilliant prose, too absorbed even to go for a swim, or take a sip of Evian. I was cured of this particular fantasy a couple of years ago, when I spent a week watching a woman on the other side of the pool reading my first novel, *High Fidelity*. Unfortunately, however, I was on holiday with my sister and brother-in-law, and my brother-in-law provided a gleeful and frankly unfraternal running commentary. "Look! Her lips are moving." "Ha! She's fallen asleep! Again!" "I talked to her in the bar last night. Not a *bright* woman, I'm afraid." At one point, alarmingly, she dropped the book and ran off. "She's gone to put out her eyes!" my brother-in-law yelled triumphantly. I was glad when she'd finished it and moved on to *Harry Potter* or Dr. Seuss or whatever else it was she'd packed.

I like to think that, once he'd recovered from the original aesthetic shock, Jonathan Lethem wouldn't have winced too often if he'd watched me reading *The Fortress of Solitude* by the pool this month. I was pinned to my lounger, and my lips hardly moved at all. In fact, I was so determined to read his novel on holiday that the first half of the reading month started with a mess. It went something like, *Being* **The** *John McEnroe* Stop-Time **Fortress of Solitude**. I'd just started Tim Adams's short book on McEnroe when an advance copy of *Fortress* came in the post, and I started reading that—but because it seemed so good, so much my kind of book, I wanted to save it, and I went back to the McEnroe. Except then the McEnroe turned out to be *too* short, and I'd finished it before the holiday started, so I needed something to fill in, which is why I reread *Stop-Time*. (And *Stop-Time* turned out to be too long, and I didn't get onto *Fortress* until the third day of the seven-day holiday.)

Last month I read a lot of Salinger, and he pops up in all three of these books. Tim Adams remembers reading *Raise High the Roof Beam, Carpenters* while queuing to watch McEnroe at Wimbledon in 1981; the seventeen-year-old Adams had a theory that McEnroe "was, in fact, a latter-day Holden Caulfield, unable and unwilling to grow up… constantly railing against the phonies—dozing linesmen, tournament organizers with walkie-talkies—in authority." Later, he points out that McEnroe went to

Buckley Country Day School—"one model for Holden Caulfield's Pencey Prep." Frank Conroy, meanwhile, attended P.S. 6, "of J. D. Salinger fame." (Adams's book is great, by the way. It's witty and smart, and has ideas about sport that don't strain for significance. It's also oddly English, because it's about the collision of McEnroe and Wimbledon—in other words, McEnroe and one version of England—and about how McEnroe was a weirdly timely illustration of Thatcherism. My favorite McEnroe tirade, one I hadn't heard before: "I'm so disgusting you shouldn't watch. Everybody leave!")

And then, at the beginning of *The Fortress of Solitude,* I came across the following, describing a street ball game: "A shot... which cleared the gates on the opposite side of the street was a home run. Henry seemed to be able to do this at will, and the fact that he didn't each time was mysterious." Compare that to this, from *Seymour: An Introduction:* "A home run was scored only when the ball sailed just high and hard enough to strike the wall of the building on the opposite street... Seymour scored a home run nearly every time he was up. When other boys on the block scored one, it was generally regarded as a fluke... but Seymour's failures to get home runs looked like flukes." Weird, huh? (And that's all it is, by the way—there's nothing sinister going on here. Lethem's book is probably over a hundred thousand words long, and bears no resemblance to anything Salinger wrote, aside from this one tiny echo.) All three books are in part about being young and mixed-up and American, and even though this would appear to be a theme so broad that no one can claim it as their own, somehow Salinger has managed to copyright it (and you wouldn't put it past him); there is clearly some law compelling you to acknowledge somewhere in your book, however obliquely, that he got there first.

A confession, for the record: I know Jonathan Lethem. Or rather, I've met him, and we have exchanged emails on occasions. But I don't know him so well that I had to read his book, if you see what I mean. I could easily have gotten away with not reading it. I could have left the proof copy his publisher sent me sitting around unopened, and no social embarrassment would have ensued. But I wanted to read it; I loved *Motherless Brooklyn,* and I knew a little bit about this book before I started it—I knew, for example, that a lot of funk records and Marvel comics were mentioned by name. In other words, it wasn't just up my street; it was actually knocking on my front door and peering through the letterbox to see if I was in. I was, however, briefly worried about the title, which sounds portentously and alarmingly Literary, until I was reminded that it refers to Superman.

The Fortress of Solitude is one of those rare novels that felt as though it had to be written; in fact, it's one of those novels that deals with something so crucial—namely, the relationship between a middle-class white boy and black culture—that you can't believe it hasn't been written before. Anyone who has grown up listening to black music, or even white music derived from black music, will have some point of connection to this book; but Dylan Ebdus, Lethem's central character, is a kind of walking, talking embodiment of a cultural obsession. He's the only white kid in his street (in Brooklyn, pre-gentrification), and one of a handful of white kids in his school; Mick Jagger would have killed for his experience, and Mick Jagger would have suffered in exactly the same ways.

This is a painful, beautiful, brave, poetic, and definitive book (anyone who attempts to enter this territory again will be found out, not least because Lethem clearly knows whereof he speaks), and though it has its flaws, the right reader will not only forgive them but love them—just as the right listener loves the flaws in, say, *The Wild, the Innocent & the E Street Shuffle.* They are the flaws that come of ambition, not of ineptitude. I think this is a book that people might argue about, but it will also be a book that a sizable number of people cherish and defend and reread, despite its density and length, and as an author you can't really ask for much more than that.

Three of the books on the "read" list—by Patrick Neate, Ian MacDonald, and Peter Guralnick—I reviewed for the *Times Literary Supplement,* and I'm not going to write about them again at any length here. But *Where You're At* is in part about a middle-class white boy's obsession with hip-hop, and *Feel Like Going Home* is fuelled by a middle-class white boy's love for R&B and blues; reading them only served to underline why *The Fortress of Solitude* is so necessary.

I do seem, however, to have spent a disproportionate amount of time reading about Stuyvesant High School this month. That's where Dylan Ebdus escapes to, and it's also where Frank Conroy went when he could be bothered. I'm guessing that Stuyvesant is decent enough, but I'm sure its students would be perplexed to hear that an Englishman spent an entire holiday in France reading about alumni both fictional and real. I even ended up checking out the Stuyvesant website, just to see what the place looked like. (It looked like a high school.)

I reread *Stop-Time* because Frank Conroy is so eloquent and moving about books and their power at the end of *Stone Reader.* I don't reread books very often; I'm too conscious of both my ignorance and my mortality. (I recently discovered that a friend who was rereading *Bleak House* had done no other Dickens apart from *Barnaby Rudge.* That's just weird. I shamed and nagged him into picking up *Great Expectations* instead.) But when I tried to recall anything about it other than its excellence, I failed. Maybe there was something about a peculiar stepfather? Or was that *This Boy's Life?* And I realized that, as this is true of just about every book I consumed between the ages of, say, fifteen and forty, I haven't even read the books I think I've read. I can't tell you how depressing this is. What's the fucking point?

Apart from Stuyvesant and Salinger, the recurring theme

of the month was Paula Fox. Fox has given blurbs for both *The Fortress of Solitude* and Zoë Heller's novel; Lethem has given a blurb to *Desperate Characters*. I know I'm wrong about this book, because everyone else in the world, including writers I love, thinks it's fantastic, but it Wasn't For Me. It's brilliantly written, I can see that much, and it made me think, too. But mostly I thought about why I don't know anyone like the people Fox writes about. Why are all my friends so dim and unreflective? Where did I go wrong?

Toward the end of the book, Otto and Sophie, the central couple, go to stay in their holiday home. Sophie opens the door to the house, and is immediately reminded of a friend, an artist who used to visit them there; she thinks about him for a page or so. The reason she's thinking about him is that she's staring at something he loved, a vinegar bottle shaped like a bunch of grapes. The reason she's staring at the bottle is because it's in pieces. And the reason it's in pieces is because someone has broken in and trashed the place, a fact we only discover when Sophie has snapped out of her reverie. At this point, I realized with some regret that not only could I never write a literary novel, but I couldn't even be a character in a literary novel. I can only imagine myself, or any character I created, saying, "Shit! Some bastard has trashed the house!" No rumination about artist friends—just a lot of cursing, and maybe some empty threats of violence.

Zoë Heller's *Notes on a Scandal,* about a fortysomething pottery teacher who has an affair with a fifteen-year-old pupil, was moving along nicely until a character starts talking about football. He tells a teaching colleague that he's been to see Arsenal, and that "Arsenal won Liverpool 3-0." Readers of this column will have realized by now that I know almost nothing about anything, but if I were forced to declare one area of expertise, it would be what people say to each other after football matches. It's not much, I know, but it's mine. And I am positive that no one has ever said "Arsenal won Liverpool 3-0" in the entire history of either

Arsenal Football Club or the English language. "Beat," "thrashed," "did" or "done," "trounced," "thumped," "shat all over," "walloped," etc., yes; "won," emphatically, no. And I think that my dismay and disbelief then led me to question other things, and the fabric of the novel started to unravel a little. Can you really find full-time pottery teachers in modern English state schools? Would a contemporary teenager really complain about being treated as "the Kunta Kinte round here" when asked to do some housework? I like Zoë Heller's writing, and this book has a terrific narrative voice that recalls Alan Bennett's work; I just wish I wasn't so picky. This is how picky I am. You know the Arsenal bit? It wasn't just the unconvincing demotic I objected to; it was the score. Arsenal haven't beaten Liverpool 3-0 at Highbury since 1991. What chance did the poor woman have?

I haven't finished the Richard Yates biography yet. I will, however, say this much: it is 613 pages long. Despite the influence Yates had on a generation of writers, it's hard enough finding people who've read the great *Revolutionary Road,* let alone people who will want to read about its author's grandparents. I propose that those intending to write a biography should first go to the National Biography Office to get a permit that tells you the number of pages you get. (There will be no right of appeal.) It's quite a simple calculation. Nobody wants to read a book longer than—what?—nine hundred pages? OK, a thousand, maybe. And you can't really get the job done in less than 250. So you're given maximum length if you're doing Dickens, say— someone who had an enormous cultural impact, wrote enormous books, and had a life outside them. And everyone else is calculated using Dickens as a yardstick. By this reckoning, Yates is a three-hundred-page man—maybe 315 tops. I'm on page 194 as we speak, and I'm going to stick with it—the book is compelling and warm and gossipy. But on page 48, I found myself reading a paragraph about the choice of gents' outfitters facing the pupils at Yates's school; I felt, personally speaking, that it could have gone.

I reread two other books this month: *How to Stop Smoking and Stay Stopped for Good,* and *Quitting Smoking—The Lazy Person's Guide!* I reread them for obvious reasons; I'll be rereading them again, too. They're good books, I think, sensible and helpful. But they're clearly not perfect. If I do stop smoking, it may be because I don't want to read Gillian Riley anymore. ✱

NOVEMBER 2003

BOOKS BOUGHT:

* *Bush at War*—Bob Woodward
* *Six Days of War*—Michael B. Oren
* *Genome*—Matt Ridley
* *Isaac Newton*—James Gleick
* *God's Pocket*—Pete Dexter
* *The Poet and the Murderer*—Simon Worrall
* *Sputnik Sweetheart*—Haruki Murakami
* *Lie Down in Darkness*—William Styron
* *Leadville*—Edward Platt
* *Master Georgie*—Beryl Bainbridge
* *How to Breathe Underwater*—Julie Orringer (two copies)

BOOKS READ:

* *A Tragic Honesty: The Life and Work of Richard Yates*—Blake Bailey (completed)
* *Wenger: The Making of a Legend*—Jasper Rees
* *How to Breathe Underwater*—Julie Orringer
* *Bush at War*—Bob Woodward (unfinished)
* Unnamed Literary Novel (abandoned)
* Unnamed Work of Nonfiction (abandoned)
* *No Name*—Wilkie Collins (unfinished)

LITERARY CDs BOUGHT AND LISTENED TO:

* *The Spoken Word*—*Poets*
* *The Spoken Word*—*Writers*

U nfinished, abandoned, abandoned, unfinished. Well, you can't say I didn't warn you. In the first of these columns, I voiced the suspicion that my then-current reading jag was unsustainable: I was worried, I seem to recall, about the end of the summer, and the forthcoming football season, and it's true that both of these factors have had an adverse effect on book consumption. (Words added to ongoing novel since autumnal return to work: not many, but more than the month before. Football matches watched in the last month: seven whole ones, four of them live in the stadium, and bits and pieces of probably half a dozen others.) Of the two books I started and finished this month, one I read in a day, mostly on a plane, during a day trip to Amsterdam. And it was a book about football.

It is not only sport and work that have slowed me up, however; I would have to say that the ethos of the *Believer* has inhibited me a little too. As you are probably aware by now, the *Believer* has taken the honorable and commendable view that, if it is attacks on contemporary writers and writing you wish to read, then you can choose from an endless range of magazines and newspapers elsewhere—just about all of them, in fact—and that therefore the *Believer* will contain only acid-free literary criticism.

This position is, however, likely to cause difficulties if your brief is simply to write honestly about the books you have been reading: Boredom and, very occasionally, despair are part of the reading life, after all. Last month, mindful of the *Believer's* raison d'être, I expressed mild disappointment with a couple of the books I had read. I don't remember the exact words; but I said something to the effect that, if I were physically compelled to express a view as to whether the Disappointing Novel was better or worse than *Crime and Punishment,* then I would keep my opinion to myself, no matter how excruciating the pain, such was my respect for the editorial credo. If, however, the torturers threatened my children, then I would—with the utmost reluctance—voice a very slight preference for *Crime and Punishment.*

Uproar ensued. Voicing a slight preference for *Crime and Punishment* over the Disappointing Novel under threat of torture to my children constituted a Snark, it appeared, and I was summoned to appear before the *Believer* committee—twelve rather eerie young men and women (six of each, naturally), all dressed in white robes and smiling maniacally, like a sort of literary equivalent of the Polyphonic Spree. I was given a severe dressing-down, and only avoided a three-issue suspension by promising never to repeat the offense. Anyway, We (i.e., the Polysyllabic Spree) have decided that if it looks as though I might not enjoy a book, I will abandon it immediately, and not mention it by name. This is what happened with the Literary Novel and the Work of Nonfiction— particularly regrettable in the latter case, as I was supposed to be reviewing it for a London newspaper. The loss of income there, and the expense of flying from London to San Francisco to face the Committee (needless to say, those bastards wouldn't stump up), means that this has been an expensive month.

I did, however, finish the biography of Richard Yates that I started last month. I haven't changed my view that it could eas- ily have afforded to shed a few of its six-hundred-plus pages— Yates doesn't sell his first story until page 133—but I'm glad I stuck with it. Who'd have thought that the author of *Revolutionary Road* wrote speeches for Robert Kennedy, or pro- vided the model for Alton Benes, the insane writer-father of *Seinfeld*'s Elaine? (Yates's daughter Monica, an ex-girlfriend of Larry David, was apparently an inspiration for Elaine herself.) And who'd have thought that the author of an acknowledged American classic, as well as several other respected novels and an outstanding collection of short stories, could have ended up living and then dying in such abject penury? *A Tragic Honesty*, like the Ian Hamilton biography of Lowell that I read recently, is a sad and occasionally terrifying account of how creativity can be simulta- neously fragile and self-destructive; it also made me grateful that I am writing now, when the antidepressants are better, and we all drink less. Stories about contemporary writers being taken away in straitjackets are thin on the ground—or no one tells them to me, anyway—but it seemed to happen to Lowell and Yates all the time; there are ten separate page references under "breakdowns" in the index of *A Tragic Honesty*.

Just as frightening to anyone who writes (or who is connected intimately to a writer) is Yates's willingness to cannibalize his life—

friends, lovers, family, work—for his fiction: Just about everyone he ever met was able to find a thinly disguised, and frequently horrific, version of themselves in a novel or a story somewhere. Those who have read *The Easter Parade* will recall the savagely-drawn portrait of Pookie, the pathetic, vain, drunken mother of the Grimes sisters; when I tell you that Yates's mother was known to everyone as "Dookie," you will understand just how far Yates was prepared to go.

It was something of a relief to turn to Jasper Rees's biography of Arsene Wenger—not just because it's short, but because Wenger's career as a football manager is currently both highly successful and unfinished. I don't often pick up books about football anymore—I wrote one once, and though the experience didn't stop me from wanting to watch the sport, as I feared it might, it did stop me from wanting to read about it—but I love Arsene, who, weirdly and neatly, coaches my team, Arsenal, and who would probably feature at about number eight in a list of People Who Have Changed My Life for the Better. He transformed a mediocre, plodding side into a thing of beauty, and on a good day, Arsenal plays the best football that anyone in England has ever seen. He was the first foreign manager to win an English championship, and his influence is such that everyone now wants to employ cool, cerebral Europeans. (The previous fashion was for ranting, red-faced Scotsmen.) Even the English national team has one now, much to the disgust of tabloid sportswriters and the more rabidly patriotic football fans.

I gave an interview to Rees for his book, but despite my contribution it's a pretty useful overview of his career to date. I couldn't, hand on heart, argue that it transcends the genre, and you probably only really need to read it if you have an Arsenal season ticket. And if there is one single *Believer* reader who is also an Arsenal season ticket holder, I'll buy you a drink next home game. What the hell—I'll buy you a car.

I received *How to Breathe Underwater* and the Wilkie Collins novel in the same Jiffy envelope, sent to me by a friend at Penguin, who publishes all three of us in the U.K.; this friend is evangelical about both books, and so I began one, loved it, finished it, and then started the other. Usually, of course, I treat personal book recommendations with the suspicion they deserve. I've got enough to read as it is, so my first reaction when someone tells me to read something is to find a way to doubt their credentials, or to try to dredge up a conflicting view from the memory. (Just as stone always blunts scissors, a lukewarm "Oh, it was OK," always beats a "You have to read this." It's less work that way.) But every now and again, the zealous gleam in someone's eye catches the attention, and anyway Joanna, jaded as she is by her work, doesn't make loose or unnecessary recommendations. She keeps her powder dry.

She was right, luckily for her: *How to Breathe Underwater* is an outstanding collection of stories. Orringer writes about the things that everyone writes about—youth, friendship, death, grief, etc.—but her narrative settings are fresh and wonderfully knotty. So, while her themes are as solid and as recognizable as oak trees, the stuff growing on the bark you've never seen before. If you wanted to be reductive, "The Smoothest Way Is Full of Stones" would collapse neatly into a coming-of-age story with a conventional two-girls-and-a-guy triangle at its core. But one of the girls comes from a ferociously orthodox Jewish family, and the other one has a mother who's in the hospital after the loss of a baby, and the boy has this pornographic book stashed away, and the whole thing is so beautifully and complicatedly imagined that you don't want to boil it down to its essence. "Pilgrims," the first story in the book, makes you feel panicky and breathless, and is destined, I suspect, to be taught in creative writing classes everywhere. The moment I'd finished I bought myself a first edition, and then another, for a friend's birthday. It's that sort of book. I'll tell you how much I liked it: One paragraph in the story "When She Is Old and I Am

Famous" contained the words "gowns," "pumps," "diva hairdos," "pink chiffon," "silk roses," "couture," and "*Vogue,*" and, after the briefest shudder, I read on anyway.

I'm a couple of hundred pages into *No Name,* and so far it's everything I'd hoped it would be. It was sold to me—or given to me free, anyway—as a lost Victorian classic (and I'd never even heard of it), and it really hits the spot: an engrossing, tortuous plot, quirky characters, pathos, the works. If you pick up the Penguin Classics edition, however, don't read the blurb on the back. It more or less blows the first (fantastic) plot twist on the grounds that it's "revealed early on"—but "early on" turns out to be page ninety-six, not, say, page eight. Note to publishers: Some people read nineteenth-century novels for fun, and a lot of them were written to be read that way too.

I should, perhaps, attempt to explain away the ludicrous number of books bought this month. Most of them were secondhand paperbacks; I bought the Pete Dexter, the Murakami, and *The Poet and the Murderer* on a Saturday afternoon spent wandering up and down Stoke Newington Church Street with the baby, and I bought *Leadville* and *Master Georgie* from a bookstall at a local community festival. *Leadville* is a biography of the A40, one of London's dreariest arterial roads, and the desperately unpromising nature of the material somehow persuades me that the book has to be great. And I'd like to point out that *The Poet and the Murderer* is the second cheap paperback about a literary hoax that I've bought since I started writing this column. I cannot really explain why I keep buying books about literary hoaxes that I never seriously intend to read. It's a quirk of character that had remained hitherto unrevealed to me.

I picked up the Styron in a remainder shop while I was reading the Yates biography—Yates spent years adapting it for a film that was never made. *Genome* and *Six Days of War* I bought on a visit to the *London Review of Books'* slightly scary new shop near the British Museum. I'm not entirely sure why I chose those two in particular, beyond the usual attempts at reinvention that periodically seize one in a bookstore. (When I'm arguing with St. Peter at the Pearly Gates, I'm going to tell him to ignore the Books Read column, and focus on the Books Bought instead. "This is *really* who I am," I'll tell him. "I'm actually much more of a *Genome* guy than an Arsene Wenger guy. And if you let me in, I'm going to prove it, honest.") I got the CDs at the *LRB* shop, too. They're actually pretty amazing: the recordings are taken from the British Library Sound Archive, and all the writers featured were born in the nineteenth century—Conan Doyle, Virginia Woolf, Joyce, Yeats, Kipling, Wodehouse, Tolkien, and, astonishingly, Browning and Tennyson, although to be honest you can't really hear Browning, who was recorded at a dinner party in 1889, trying and failing to remember the words of "How They Brought the Good News from Ghent to Aix." Weirdly, everyone sounds the same: very posh and slightly mad.

I read about a third of *Bush at War*, and I may well return to it at some stage, but the mood that compelled me to begin it passed quickly, and in any case it wasn't quite what I wanted: Woodward's tone is way too matey and sympathetic for me. I did, however, learn that George W. Bush was woken up by the Secret Service at 11:08 p.m. on 9/11. Woken up! He didn't work late that night? And he wasn't too buzzy to get off to sleep? See, if that had been me, I would have been up until about six, drinking and smoking and watching TV, and I would have been useless the next day. It can't be right, can it, that world leaders emerge not through their ability to solve global problems, but to nod off at the drop of a hat? Most decent people can't sleep easily at night, and that, apparently, is precisely why the world is in such a mess. ✷

DECEMBER 2003
& JANUARY 2004

BOOKS BOUGHT:
* *Moneyball*—Michael Lewis
* *Saul and Patsy*—Charles Baxter
* *Winner of the National Book Award*—Jincy Willett
* *Jenny and the Jaws of Life*—Jincy Willett
* *The Sirens of Titan*—Kurt Vonnegut
* *True Notebooks*—Mark Salzman

BOOKS READ:
* *No Name*—Wilkie Collins
* *Moneyball*—Michael Lewis
* *George and Sam: Autism in the Family*—Charlotte Moore
* *The Sirens of Titan*—Kurt Vonnegut

First, an apology. Last month, I may have inadvertently given the impression that *No Name* by Wilkie Collins was a lost Victorian classic (the misunderstanding may have arisen because of my loose use of the phrase "lost Victorian classic"), and that everyone should rush out and buy it. I had read over two hundred pages when I gave you my considered verdict; in fact, the last four hundred and eighteen pages nearly killed me, and I wish I were speaking figuratively. We fought, Wilkie Collins and I. We fought bitterly and with all our might, to a standstill, over a period of about three weeks, on trains and airplanes and by hotel swimming pools. Sometimes—usually late at night, in bed—he could put me out cold with a single paragraph; every time I got through twenty or thirty pages, it felt to me as though I'd socked him good, but it took a lot out of me, and I had to retire to my corner to wipe the blood and sweat off my reading glasses. And still he kept coming back for more. Only in the last fifty-odd pages, after I'd landed several of these blows, did old Wilkie show any signs of buckling under the assault. He was pretty tough for a man of nearly one hundred and eighty. Hats off to him. Anyway, I'm sorry for the bum steer, and readers of this column insane enough to have run down to their nearest bookstore as a result of my advice should write to the *Believer,* enclosing a receipt, and we will refund your $14. It has to say *No Name* on the receipt, though, because we weren't born yesterday, and we're not stumping up for your Patricia Cornwell novels. You can pay for them yourselves.

In his introduction to my Penguin edition, Mark Ford points out that Collins wrote the closing sections of the novel "in both great pain and desperate anxiety over publishers' deadlines." (In fact, Dickens, who edited the magazine in which *No Name* was originally published, *All the Year Round,* offered to nip down to London and finish the book off for him: "I could take it up any time and do it… so like you as that no-one should find out the difference." That's literature for you.) It is not fair to wonder why Collins bothered: *No Name* has lots going for it, including a driven, complicated, and morally ambiguous central female character, and a tremendous first two hundred pages. But it's certainly reasonable to wonder why a sick man should have wanted to overextend a relatively slight melodrama to the extent that people want to fight him. *No Name* is the story of a woman's attempt to reclaim her rightful inheritance from cruel and heartless relatives, and one of the reasons the book didn't work for me is that one has to quiver with outrage throughout at the prospect of this poor girl having to work for a living, as a governess or something equally demeaning.

It could be, of course, that the book seems bloated because Collins simply wasn't as good at handling magazine serialization as Dickens, and that huge chunks of the novel, which originally came in forty-four parts, were written only to keep the end well away from the beginning. I'm only guessing, but I'd imagine that many subscribers to *All the Year Round* between May 1862 and early January 1863 felt exactly the same way. I'm guessing, in fact, that there were a few cancelled subscriptions, and that *No Name* is the chief reason you can no longer find *All the Year Round* alongside the *Believer* at your nearest newsstand.

There are two sides to every fight, though, and Wilkie would point out that I unwisely attempted to read the second half of *No Name* during a trip to L.A. Has anyone ever attempted a Victorian novel in Los Angeles, and if so, why? In England, we read Victorian novels precisely because they're long, and we have nothing else to do. L.A. is too warm, too bright, there's too much sport on TV, and the sandwiches are too big (and come with chips/"fries"). English people shouldn't attempt to do anything in L.A.; it's all too much. We should just lie in a darkened room with a cold flannel until it's time to come home again.

With the exception of *The Sirens of Titan,* bought secondhand from a Covent Garden market stall, all this month's books were purchased at Book Soup in L.A. (Book Soup and the Tower Records directly opposite have become, in my head, what Los Angeles *is*.) Going to a good U.S. bookshop is still ludicrously exciting—unless I'm on book tour, when the excitement tends to wear off a little. As I don't see American books-pages, I have no idea whether one of my favorite authors—Charles Baxter, for example, on this trip—has a new book out, and there's every chance that it won't be published in the U.K. for months, if at all. There is enough money in the music and movie industries to ensure that we get to hear about most things that might interest us; books have to remain a secret, to be discovered only when you spend time browsing. This is bad for authors, but good for the assiduous shopper.

Mark Salzman's book about juvenile offenders I read about in the *Believer*. I met Mark after a reading in L.A. some years ago, and one of the many memorable things he told me was that he'd written a large chunk of his last novel almost naked, covered in aluminum foil, with a towel round his head, sitting in a car. His reasons for doing so, which I won't go into here, were sound, and none of them were connected with mental illness, although perhaps inevitably he had caused his wife some embarrassment—especially when she brought friends back to the house. Jincy Willett, whose work I had never heard of, I bought because of her blurbs, which, I'm afraid to say, only goes to show that blurbs do work.

I was in the U.S. for the two epic playoff series, between the Cubs and the Marlins, and the Red Sox and the Yankees, and I became temporarily fixated with baseball. And I'd read something about *Moneyball* somewhere, and it was a staff pick at Book Soup, and when, finally, *No Name* lay vanquished and lifeless at my feet, it was Lewis's book I turned to: it seemed a better fit. *Moneyball* is a rotten title, I think. You expect a subtitle something along the lines of *How Greed Killed America's National Pastime,* but actually the book isn't like that at all—it's the story of how Billy Beane, the GM of the Oakland A's, worked out how to buck the system and win lots of games despite being hampered by one of the smallest payrolls in baseball. He did this by recognizing (*a*) that the stats traditionally used to judge players are almost entirely worthless, and (*b*) that many good players are being discarded by the major leagues simply because they don't *look* like good players.

The latter discovery in particular struck a chord with me, because my football career has been blighted by exactly this sort of prejudice. English scouts visiting my Friday morning five-a-side game have (presumably) discounted me on peripheral grounds of age, weight, speed, amount of time spent lying on the ground weeping with exhaustion, etc.; what they're not looking at is *performance,* which is of course the only thing that counts. They'd have made a film called *Head It Like Hornby* by now if Billy Beane were working over here. (And if I were any good at heading, another overrated and peripheral skill.) Anyway, I understood about one word in every four of *Moneyball,* and it's still the best and most engrossing sports book I've read in years. If you know anything about baseball, you will enjoy it four times as much as I did, which means that you might explode.

I have an autistic son, but I don't often read any books about autism. Most of the time, publishers seem to want to hear from or about autists with special talents, as in *Rain Man* (my son, like the vast majority of autistic kids and contrary to public perception, has no special talent, unless you count his remarkable ability to hear the opening of a crisp packet from several streets away), or from parents who believe that they have "rescued" or "cured" their autistic child (and there is no cure for autism, although there are a few weird stories, none of which seem applicable to my son's condition). So most books on the subject tend to make me feel alienated, resentful, cynical, or simply baffled. Granted, pretty much any book on any subject seems to make me feel this way, but I reckon that in this case, my personal experience of the subject means I'm entitled to feel anything I want.

I read Charlotte Moore's book because I agreed to write an introduction for it, and I agreed to write an introduction because, in a series of brilliant columns in the *Guardian,* she has managed not only to tell it like it is, but to do so with enormous good humor and wit—*George and Sam* (Moore has three sons, two of whom are autistic) is, believe it or not, the funniest book I've read this year. I'm not sure I would have found it as funny six or seven years ago, when Danny was first diagnosed and autism wasn't a topic that made me laugh much; but now that I'm used to glancing out of the window on cold wet November nights and suddenly seeing a ten-year-old boy bouncing naked and gleeful on a trampoline, I have come to relish the stories all parents of autistic kids have.

The old cliché "You couldn't make it up" is always dispiriting to anyone who writes fiction—if you couldn't make it up, then it's probably not worth talking or writing about anyway. But autism is worth writing about—not just because it affects an increasingly large number of people, but because of the light the condition shines down on the rest of us. And though you can predict that autistic kids are likely to behave in peculiar obsessive-compulsive ways, the details of these compulsions and obsessions are always completely unimaginable and frequently charming in their strangeness. Sam, the younger of Moore's two autistic boys, has an obsession with oasthouses—he once escaped from home in order to explore a particularly fine example a mile and a half away. "Its owner, taking an afternoon nap, was startled to be joined in bed by a small boy still wearing his Wellington boots."

George, meanwhile, is compelled to convince everyone that he doesn't eat, even though he does. After his mum has made his breakfast she has to reassure him that it's for Sam, and then turn her back until he's eaten it. (Food has to be smuggled into school, hidden inside his swimming things.) Sam loves white goods, especially washing machines, so during a two-week stay in London he was taken to a different launderette each day, and nearly combusted with excitement; he also likes to look at bottles of lavatory cleaner through frosted glass. George parrots lines he's learned from videotapes: "The Government has let me down," he told his trampoline teacher recently. (For some reason, trampolines are a big part of our lives.) "This would make Ken Russell spit with envy," he remarked enigmatically on another occasion. Oasthouses, washing machines, pretending not to eat when really you do... see? You really couldn't make it up.

I don't want to give the impression that living with an autistic child is *all* fun. If you have a child of the common or garden-variety, I wouldn't recommend, on balance, that you swap him in (most autistic kids are boys) for a child with a hilarious obsession. Hopefully I need hardly add that there's some stuff that... well, that, to understate the case, isn't quite as hilarious. I am merely pointing out, as Moore is doing, that if you are remotely interested in the strangeness and variety and beauty of humankind, then there is a lot in the condition to marvel at. This is the first book about autism I've read that I'd recommend to people who want to know what it is like; it's sensible about education, diet, possible causes, just about everything that affects the quotidian lives of those dealing with the condition. It also made this parent feel better about the compromises one has to make: "This morning George breakfasted on six After Eights [After Eights are "sophisticated" chocolate mints] and some lemon barley-water. I was pleased—*pleased*—because lately he hasn't been eating at all..." In our house it's salt-and-vinegar crisps.

I can imagine *George and Sam* doing a roaring trade with grandparents, aunts, and uncles tough enough to want to know the truth. I read it while listening to Damien Rice's beautiful *O* for the first time, and I had an unexpectedly transcendent moment: the book colored the music, and the music colored the book, and I ended up feeling unambivalently happy that my son is who he is; those moments are precious. I hope *George and Sam* finds a U.S. publisher.

A couple of months ago, I became depressed by the realization that I'd forgotten pretty much everything I've ever read. I have, however, bounced back: I am now cheered by the realization that if I've forgotten everything I've ever read then I can read some of my favorite books again *as if for the first time*. I remembered the punch line of *The Sirens of Titan,* but everything else was as fresh as a daisy, and Vonnegut's wise, lovely, world-weary novel was a perfect way to cap Charlotte Moore's book: she'd prepared the way beautifully for a cosmic and absurdly reductive view of our planet. I'm beginning to see that our appetite for books is the same as our appetite for food, that our brain tells us when we need the literary equivalent of salads, or chocolate, or meat and potatoes. When I read *Moneyball*, it was because I wanted something quick and light after the 32-oz steak of *No Name*; *The Sirens of Titan* wasn't a reaction against *George and Sam*, but a way of enhancing it. So what's that? Mustard? MSG? A brandy? It went down a treat, anyway.

Smoking is rubbish, most of the time. But if I'd never smoked, I'd never have met Kurt Vonnegut. We were both at a huge party in New York, and I sneaked out onto the balcony for a cigarette, and there he was, smoking. So we talked—about C. S. Forester, I seem to remember. (That's just a crappy and phony figure of speech. Of course I remember.) So tell your kids not to smoke, but it's only fair to warn them of the downside, too: that they will therefore never get the chance to offer the greatest living writer in America a light. ✷

A selection from

GEORGE AND SAM: AUTISM IN THE FAMILY

by **CHARLOTTE MOORE**

★ ★ ★

Monday morning. We're in a hurry—of course we are. Every working mother with three school-age sons is in a hurry on a Monday morning.

George is nearly thirteen. The physical process of puberty is beginning, but he seems unaware of this, just as he's always been unaware of the effect his exceptional good looks have on people. He wanders into the kitchen, naked. He climbs on to the Aga, and sits there twiddling a piece of cardboard. I send him to get dressed; his skin is red and mottled from the heat. He returns with all his clothes on the wrong way round.

I fill a lunchbox for eleven-year-old Sam. Plain crisps, gluten-free biscuits, marzipan, an apple that I know he won't eat, but I suppose I live on in hope. George doesn't have a lunchbox, because George maintains the fiction that he doesn't eat anything at all, and a lunchbox is too blatant a reminder that this cannot be the case. I smuggle his food supplies—mainly Twiglets and chocolate—into his school taxi, underneath his swimming things.

I make George's breakfast—but I have to pretend it's not his breakfast. "I'm making this for Sam," I announce, pointedly. I toast two slices of rice bread; Sam's diet excludes wheat, oats, barley, rye and all dairy products. I place them on two plates which George has selected by sniffing. I spread Marmite in an even layer right up to the edge of the crusts, cut them into quarters, then busy myself elsewhere. George slips down from the Aga; as long as my back's

45

turned, he'll risk the toast. "These are for Sam," he states as he starts to eat. "Yes, they're for Sam," I confirm, without looking round.

Sam's always the last up. He's awake, but he's under his duvet, murmuring; his vocalization is somewhere between a hum and a chant, and is almost completely incomprehensible. He fingers the toy owl he's had since babyhood. The owl has no name, no character; Sam has never played with him, but then, he's rarely played with any toy. The owl is a tactile comforter, not a friend.

Sam won't get up and dress until the taxi driver rings the doorbell. I did try ringing it myself, to get him moving, but Sam's not daft. He only fell for that once. And the dressing process can be infuriatingly slow. Pants on—pants off again. Shirt inside out—outside in—inside out once more. Six pairs of identical tracksuit trousers rejected—the seventh finally, mysteriously, acceptable. Socks stuffed down into the toes of his trainers, pulled out, stuffed in again. One step forward, two steps back—and endless little rituals about touching things and moving things in his bedroom. If I try to intervene, the whole process starts all over again.

At last he's dressed—no time for niceties like washing or brushing teeth. Now Sam has to get down the stairs all in one go. If anything blocks his way, or if he has a crisis of confidence halfway down, he'll freeze. He takes the stairs at a gallop, gets as far as the front door. I open the door for him. Mistake! Sam has to do everything for himself. He opens and shuts the door six times before he can bring himself to leave the house.

George's taxi arrives. I note with pleasure that the toast has been eaten—but where is George? In the lavatory of course, where he spends about a quarter of his waking hours. He emerges, and makes for the front door—but wait, there's something odd about his gait. He's pulled up his trousers, but forgotten about his pants. I ignore his protests, hoick up his pants, waft a brush over his uncut hair, and propel him towards the taxi. "Don't wave! Don't say goodbye!" he commands, and hands me a fragment of sweet paper to add to the collection that already covers the kitchen table. Two empty Fanta bottles, eight yellow lollipop sticks, silver foil, Softmint wrappers... hoarding litter is George's latest obsession.

A call from the playroom reminds me of the existence of my youngest child. *Blue Peter* has finished; Jake, four, wants his Ready Brek. He chats as he eats; he'd like to meet Gareth Gates, he'd like to be Young Sportsman of the Year. Have I found his reading book? Can he have three kinds of sugar on his cereal?

I take Jake to the local primary school, where he is in Reception. He greets his friends on the way in, dismisses me with a hug and a kiss. Neither George nor Sam ever embrace me in greeting or salute.

As I leave, I peep through the window. Jake is cross-legged in the middle of the group; he is listening to what the teacher has to say. His hand shoots up. He's right in there, a proper schoolboy, a social animal. He couldn't be more different from his older brothers—but then, Jake's not autistic. ✶

FEBRUARY 2004

My first book was published just over eleven years ago and remains in print, and though I observed the anniversary with only a modest celebration (a black-tie dinner for forty of my closest friends, many of whom were kind enough to read out the speeches I had prepared for them), I can now see that I should have made more of a fuss: in *Enemies of Promise,* which was written in 1938, the critic Cyril Connolly attempts to isolate the qualities that make a book last for ten years.

Over the decades since its publication, *Enemies of Promise* has been reduced pretty much to one line: "There is no more sombre enemy of good art than the pram in the hall," which is possibly why I was never previously very interested in reading it. What are you supposed to do if the pram in the hall is already there? You could move it out into the garden, I suppose, if you have a garden, or get rid of it and carry the little bastards everywhere, but maybe I'm being too literal-minded.

Enemies of Promise is about a lot more than the damaging effects of domesticity, however; it's also about prose style, and the perils of success, and journalism, and politics. Anyone who writes, or wants to write, will find something on just about every single page that either endorses a long-held prejudice or outrages, and that makes it a pretty compelling read. Ironically, the copy I found on the shelf belongs to one of the mothers of my children. I wonder if she knew, when she bought it twenty years ago, that she would one day partially destroy a literary career? Connolly would probably argue that she did. He generally takes a pretty dim view of women, who "make crippling demands on [a writer's] time and money, especially if they set their hearts on his popular success." Bless 'em, eh? I'm presuming, as Connolly does, that you're a man. What would a woman be doing reading a literary magazine anyway?

Connolly spends the first part of the book dividing writers into two camps, the Mandarin and the Vernacular. (He is crankily thorough in this division, by the way. He even goes through the big books of the twenties year by year, and marks them with a V or an M: "1929—H. Green, *Living* (V); W. Faulkner, *The Sound and the Fury* (M); Hemingway, *A Farewell to Arms* (V); Lawrence, *Pansies* (V); Joyce, *Fragments of a Work in Progress* (M)," and so on. One hesitates to point it out—it's too late now—but shouldn't Connolly have been getting on with his writing, rather than fiddling around with lists? That's one of your enemies, right there.) And then, having thus divided, he spends a lot of time despairing of both camps. "The Mandarin style... is beloved of literary pundits, by those who would make the written word as unlike as possible to the spoken one. It is the title of those writers whose tendency is to make their language convey more than they mean or more than they feel." (Yay, Cyril! Way to go!) Meanwhile, "According to Gide, a good writer should navigate against the current; the practitioners in the new vernacular are swimming with it; the familiarities of the advertisements in the morning paper, the matey leaders in the *Daily Express,* the blather of the film critics, the wisecracks of the newsreel commentators, the know-all autobiographies of political reporters, the thrillers and 'teccies... are all swimming with it too." (Cyril, you utter *ass*. You think Hemingway wrote like that lot? Have another look, mate.) Incidentally, the "know-all autobiographies of political reporters"—that was a whole *genre* in the nineteen-thirties? Boy.

The invention of paperbacks, around the time Connolly was writing *Enemies of Promise,* changed everything. Connolly's ten-year question could fill a book in 1938 because the answer was genuinely complicated then; books really could sit out the vicissitudes of fashion on library shelves, and then dust themselves off and climb back down into readers' laps. Paperbacks and chain bookstores mean that a contemporary version of *Enemies of Promise* would consist of one simple and uninteresting question: "Well, did it sell in its first year?" My first book did OK; meanwhile, books that I reviewed and loved in 1991 and 1992, books every bit as good or better than mine, are out of print, simply because they never found a readership then. They might have passed all the Connolly tests, but they're dead in the water anyway.

You end up muttering back at just about every ornately constructed *pensée* that Connolly utters, but that's one of the joys of this book. At one point, he strings together a few sentences by Hemingway, Isherwood, and Orwell in an attempt to prove that their prose styles are indistinguishable. But the point, surely, is that though you can make Connolly's sentence-by-sentence case easily enough, you'd never confuse a book by Orwell with a book by Hemingway—and that's what they were doing, writing books. Look, here's a plain, flat, vernacular sentence:

> So I bought a little city (it was Galveston, Texas) and told everybody that nobody had to move, we were going to do it just gradually, very relaxed, no big changes overnight.

This is the tremendous first line of Donald Barthelme's story "I Bought a Little City" (V); one fears that Connolly might have spent a lot of time looking at the finger, and ignored what it was pointing at. ("See, he bought a whole *city*, Cyril! Galveston, Texas! Oh, forget it.") The vernacular turned out to be far more adaptable than Connolly could have predicted.

Reading the book now means that one can, if one wants, play Fantasy Literature—match writers off against each other and see who won over the long haul. (M) or (V)? Faulkner or Henry Green? I reckon the surprise champ was P. G. Wodehouse, as elegant and resourceful a prose stylist as anyone held up for our inspection here; Connolly is sniffy about him several times over the course of *Enemies of Promise,* and presumes that his stuff won't last five minutes, but he has turned out to be as enduring as anyone apart from Orwell. Jokes, you see. People do like jokes.

The Polysyllabic Spree, the twelve terrifyingly beatific young men and woman who run the *Believer,* have been quiet of late—they haven't been giving me much trouble, anyway. A friend who works in the same building has heard the ominous rustle of white robes upstairs, however, and he reckons they're planning something pretty big, maybe something like another Jonestown. (That makes sense, if you think about it. The robes, the eerie smiles, "the *Believer*"... if you find a free sachet of powdered drink, or—more likely—an edible poem in this month's issue, don't touch it.) Anyway, while they're thus distracted, I shall attempt to sneak a snark under the wire: Tobias Wolff's *Old School* is too short. Oh, come on, guys! That's different from saying it's too long! Too long means you didn't like it! Too short means you did!

The truth is, I've been reading more short books recently because I need to bump up the numbers in the Books Read column—six of this month's seven were really pretty scrawny. But *Old School* I would have read this month, the month of its publication, no matter how long it was: Wolff's two volumes of memoir, *This Boy's Life* and *In Pharaoh's Army*, are perennial sources of writerly inspiration, and you presumably know how good his stories are. *Old School* is brilliant—painful, funny, exquisitely written, acute about writers and literary ambition. (*Old School* is set right at the beginning of the sixties, in a boys' private school, and you get to meet Robert Frost and Ayn Rand.) But the problem with short novels is that you can take liberties with them: you know you're going to get through them no matter what, so you never set aside the time or the commitment that a bigger book requires. I fucked *Old School* up; I should have read it in a sitting, but I didn't, and I never gave it a chance to leave its mark. We are never allowed to forget that some books are badly written; we should remember that sometimes they're badly read, too.

Eats, Shoots and Leaves (the title refers to a somewhat labored joke about a misplaced comma and a panda) is Britain's number-one best seller at the moment, and it's about punctuation, and no, I don't get it, either. It's a sweet, good-humored book, and it's grammatically sound and all, but, you know… it really is all about how to use a semicolon and all that. What's going on? One writer I know suspects that the book's enormous success is due to the disturbing rise of the Provincial Pedant, but I have a more benign theory: that when you hear about it (and you hear about it a lot, at the moment), you think of someone immediately, someone you know and love, whose punctuation exasperates you and fills them full of self-loathing. I thought of Len, and my partner thought of

Emily, neither of whom could place an apostrophe correctly if their lives depended on it. (Names have been changed, by the way, to protect the semiliterate.) And I'm sure Len and Emily will receive a thousand copies each for Christmas and birthdays, and other people will buy a thousand copies for their Lens and Emilys, and in the end the book will sell a quarter of a million copies, *but only two hundred different people will own them.* I enjoyed the fearful bashing that Lynn Truss gives to the entertainment industry—the Hugh Grant movie *Two Weeks Notice* (sic), *Who Framed Roger Rabbit* (sic), the fabricated English pop band Hear'Say (sic)—and the advice she quotes from a newspaper style manual: "Punctuation is a courtesy designed to help readers understand a story without stumbling," which helps to explain a lot of literary fiction. I had never before heard of the Oxford comma (used before the "and" that brings a list to a close), and I didn't know that Jesus never gets a possessive "s," just because of who He is. I never really saw the possessive "s" as profane, or even very secular, but there you go.

The most irritating book of the month (can't you feel the collective heart of the Spree beating a little faster?) was Joe Pernice's *Meat Is Murder.* One can accept, reluctantly, Pernice's apparently inexhaustible ability to knock out brilliant three-minute pop songs—just about any Pernice Brothers record contains half a dozen tunes comparable to Elvis Costello's best work. But now it turns out that he can write fiction too, and so envy and bitterness become unavoidable. *Meat Is Murder* and Warren Zanes's *Dusty in Memphis* are both part of a new and neat little "33 ⅓" series published by Continuum; Pernice is the only writer who has chosen to write a novella about a favorite album, rather than an essay; his story is set in 1985, and is about high school and suicide and teen depression and, tangentially, the Smiths. Warren Zanes's effort, almost the polar opposite of Pernice's, is a long, scholarly and convincing piece of nonfiction analyzing the myth of the American

South. Endearingly, neither book mentions the relevant records as much as you'd expect: the music is a ghostly rather than physical presence. I liked Art Linson's *What Just Happened?*, one of those scabrous, isn't-Hollywood-awful books written by someone—a producer, in this case (and indeed in most other cases, e.g. Julia Phillips, Lynda Obst)—who knows what he's talking about. I can't really explain why I picked it up, however; perhaps I wanted to be made grateful that I work in publishing, rather than film, and that's what happened.

Clockers was my big book of the month, the centerpiece around which I can now arrange the short books so that they look functional—pretty, even, if I position them right. I cheated a little, I know—*Clockers* is essentially a thriller, so it didn't feel as though I'd had to work for my 650 pages—but it was still a major reading job. Why isn't Richard Price incredibly famous, like Tom Wolfe? His work is properly plotted, indisputably authentic and serious-minded, and it has soul and moral authority.

Clockers asks—almost in passing, and there's a lot more to it than this—a pretty interesting question: if you choose to work for the minimum wage when everyone around you is pocketing thousands from drug deals, then what does that do to you, to your head and to your heart? Price's central characters, brothers Strike (complicatedly bad, a crack dealer) and Victor (complicatedly good, the minimum wage guy), act out something that feels as inevitable and as durable as a Bible story, except with a lot more swearing and drugs. *Clockers* is—eek—really about the contradictions of capitalism.

I've been trying to write a short story that entails my knowing something about contemporary theories of time—hence *Introducing Time*—but every time I pick up any kind of book about science I start to cry. This actually inhibits my reading pretty badly, due to not being able to see. I'm OK with time theorists up until, say, St. Augustine, and then I start to panic, and the panic then gives way to actual weeping. By my estimation, I should be able to understand Newton by the time I'm 850 years old—by which time I'll probably discover that some smartass has invented a new theory, and he's out of date anyway. The short story should be done some time shortly after that. Anyway, I hope you enjoy it, because it's killing me. ✷

MARCH 2004

So this last month was, as I believe you people say, a bust. I had high hopes for it, too; it was Christmastime in England, and I was intending to do a little holiday comfort reading—*David Copperfield* and a couple of John Buchan novels, say, while sipping an eggnog and heroically ploughing my way through some enormous animal carcass or other. I've been a father for ten years now, and not once have I been able to sit down and read several hundred pages of Dickens during the Christmas holidays. Why I thought it might be possible this year, now that I have twice as many children, is probably a question best discussed with an analyst—somewhere along the line, I have failed to take something on board. (Hey, great idea: if you have kids, give your partner reading vouchers next Christmas. Each voucher entitles the bearer to two hours' reading-time *while kids are awake*. It might look like a cheapskate present, but parents will appreciate that it costs more in real terms than a Lamborghini.)

If I'm honest, however, it wasn't just snot-nosed children who crawled between and all over me and Richard Hannay. One of the reasons I wanted to write this column, I think, is because I assumed that the cultural highlight of my month would arrive in book form, and that's true, for probably eleven months of the year. Books are, let's face it, better than everything else. If we played Cultural Fantasy Boxing League, and made books go fifteen rounds in the ring against the best that any other art form had to offer, then books would win pretty much every time. Go on, try it. "The Magic Flute" v. *Middlemarch*? *Middlemarch* in six. "The Last Supper" v. *Crime and Punishment*? Fyodor on points. See? I mean, I don't know how scientific this is, but it feels like the novels are walking it. You might get the occasional exception—"Blonde on Blonde" might mash up *The Old Curiosity Shop*, say, and I wouldn't give much for *Pale Fire*'s chances against *Citizen Kane*. And every now and again you'd get a shock, because that happens in sport, so *Back to the Future III* might land a lucky punch on *Rabbit, Run*; but I'm still backing literature twenty-nine times out of thirty. Even if you love movies and music as much as you do books, it's still, in any given four-week period, way, *way* more likely you'll find a great book you haven't read than a great movie you haven't seen, or a great album you haven't heard: the assiduous consumer will eventually exhaust movies and music. Sure, there will always be gaps and blind spots, but I've been watching and listening for a long time, and I'll never again have the feeling everyone has with literature: that we can't get through the good novels published in the last six months, let alone those published since publishing began. This month, however, the cultural highlight was a rock-and-roll show—two shows, actually, one of which took place in a pub called the Fiddler's Elbow in Kentish Town, North London. The Fiddler's Elbow is not somewhere you would normally expect to find your most memorable drink of the month, let alone your most memorable spiritual moment, but there you go: God really is everywhere. Anyway, against all the odds, and even though they were fighting above their weight, these shows punched the books to the floor. And they were good books, too.

Five or six years ago, a friend in Philly introduced me to a local band called Marah. Their first album had just come out, on an indie label, and it sounded great to me, like the Pogues reimagined by the E Street Band, full of fire and tunes and soul and banjos. There was a buzz about it, and they got picked up by Steve Earle's label, E-Squared; their next album got noticed by Greil Marcus and Stephen King (who proudly wore a Marah T-shirt in a photo-shoot) and Springsteen himself, and it looked like they were off and away. Writing this down, I can suddenly see the reason why it didn't happen for them, or at least, why it hasn't happened yet. Steve Earle, Stephen King, Greil Marcus, Bruce, me... none of us is under a hundred years old. The band is young, but their refer-ents, the music they love, is getting on a bit, and in an attempt to address this problem, they attempted to alienate their ancient fans with a noisy modern rock album. They succeeded in the alien-ation, but not in finding a new audience, so they have been forced to retreat and retrench and rethink. At the end of the Fiddler's Elbow show they passed a hat around, which gives you some indi-cation of the level of retrenchment going on. They'll be OK. Their next album will be a big hit, and they'll sell out Madison Square Garden, and you'll all be boasting that you read a column by a guy who saw them in the Fiddler's Elbow.

Anyway, the two shows I saw that week were spectacular, as

good as anything I've seen with the possible exception of the
Clash in '79, Prince in '85, and Springsteen on the *River* tour.
Dave and Serge, the two brothers who are to Marah what the
Gallaghers are to Oasis, played the Fiddler's Elbow as if it were
Giants Stadium, and even though it was acoustic, they just about
blew the place up. They were standing on chairs and lying on the
floor, they were funny, they charmed everyone in the pub apart
from an old drunk sitting next to the drum kit (a drummer turned
up halfway through the evening with his own set, having played a
gig elsewhere first), who put his fingers firmly in his ears during
Serge's extended harmonica solo. (His mate, meanwhile, rose
unsteadily to his feet and started clapping along.) It was utterly
bizarre and very moving: most musicians wouldn't have bothered
turning up, let alone almost killing themselves. And I was reminded—and this happened the last time I saw them play, too—
how rarely one feels included in a live show. Usually you watch,
and listen, and drift off, and the band plays well or doesn't and it
doesn't matter much either way. It can actually be a very lonely
experience. But I felt a part of the music, and a part of the people
I'd gone with, and, to cut this short before the encores, I didn't
want to read for about a fortnight afterward. I wanted to write, but
I couldn't because of the holidays, and I wanted to listen to Marah,
but I didn't want to read no book. I was too itchy, too energized,
and if young people feel like that every night of the week, then,
yes, literature's dead as a dodo. (In an attempt to get myself back
on course, I bought Bill Ehrhardt's book *Vietnam-Perkasie,* because
he comes Marah-endorsed, and provided the inspiration for
"Round Eye Blues," one of their very best songs. I didn't read the
thing, though. And their next album is tentatively entitled *20,000
Streets Under the Sky,* after a Patrick Hamilton novel—I'm going to
order that and not read it, too.)

   It wasn't as if I didn't try; it was just that very little I picked
up fit very well with my mood. I bought Flaubert's letters after

reading the piece about Donald Barthelme's required reading list in the *Believer* [October, 2003], but they weren't right—or at least, they're not if one chooses to read them in chronological order. The young Flaubert wasn't very rock and roll. He was, on this evidence, kind of a prissy, nerdy kid. "friend, I shall send you some of my political speeches, liberal constitutionalist variety," he wrote to Ernest Chevalier in January 1831; he'd just turned nine years old. Nine! Get a life, kid! (Really? You wrote those? They're pretty good books. Well… Get another one, then.) I am probably taking more pleasure than is seemly in his failure to begin the sentence with a capital letter. You know, as in, Jesus, he didn't know the first thing about basic punctuation! How did this loser ever get to be a writer?

Francis Wheen's *How Mumbo-Jumbo Conquered the World* was a better fit, because, well, it rocks: it's fast and smart and very funny, despite being about how we have betrayed the Enlightenment by retreating back to the Dark Ages. Wheen wrote a warm, witty biography of Marx a few years back and has a unique, sharp, enviable, and trustworthy mind. Here he dishes it out two-fisted to Tony Blair and George W. Bush, Deepak Chopra and Francis Fukuyama, Princess Diana and Margaret Thatcher, Hillary Clinton and Jacques Derrida, and by the end of the book you do have the rather dizzying sensation that you, the author, and maybe Richard Dawkins are the only remotely sane people in the entire world. It's difficult to endorse this book without committing a few cardinal *Believer* sins: as you may have noticed, some of the people that Wheen accuses of talking bullshit are, regrettably, writers, and in a chapter entitled "The Demolition Merchants of Reality," Wheen lumps deconstructionism in with creationism. In other words, he claims there isn't much to choose from between Pat Buchanan and Jacques Lacan when it comes to mumbo-jumbo, and I'm sorry to say that I laughed a lot. The next chapter, "The Catastrophists," gives homeopathy, astrology, and UFOlogy a good kicking, and you'll find yourself conveniently forgetting the month you gave up coffee and mint because you were taking arnica three times a day. (Did you know that Jacques Benveniste, one of the world's leading homeopathic "scientists," now claims that you can *email* homeopathic remedies? Yeah, see, what you do is you can take the "memory" of the diluted substance out of the water electromagnetically, put it on your computer, email it, and play it back on a sound card into new water. I mean, that could work, right?)

Richard Dawkins, Wheen recalls, once pointed out that if an alternative remedy proves to be efficacious—that is to say, if it is shown to have curative properties in rigorous medical trials—then "it ceases to be an alternative; it simply becomes medicine." In other words, it's only "alternative" so long as it's been shown not to be any bloody good. I found it impossible not to apply this helpful observation to other areas of life. Maybe a literary novel is just a novel that doesn't really work, and an art film merely a film that people don't want to see… *How Mumbo-Jumbo Conquered the World* is a clever-clogs companion to Michael Moore's *Stupid White Men*; and as it's about people of both sexes and every conceivable hue, it's arguably even more ambitious.

I read *Liar's Poker,* Michael Lewis's book about bond-traders in the eighties, for two reasons, one of which was Wheen-inspired: he made me want to try and be more clever, especially about grown-up things like economics. Plus I'd read Lewis's great *Moneyball* a couple of months previously [see p. 40], so I already knew that he was capable of leading me through the minefields of my own ignorance. It turns out, though, that the international money markets are more complicated than baseball. These guys buy and sell mortgages! They buy and sell risk! But I haven't got a clue what any of that actually means! This isn't Michael Lewis's fault—he really did try his best, and in any case you kind of romp through the book anyway: the people are pretty compelling, if completely unlike anyone you might meet in real life. At one point, Lewis

describes an older trader throwing a ten-dollar bill at a young colleague about to take a business flight. "Hey, take out some crash
insurance for yourself in my name," the older guy says. "I feel
lucky." As a metaphor for what happens on the trading floor, that's
pretty hard to beat.

· Francis Wheen's book and Paul Collins's *Not Even Wrong* were
advance reading copies that arrived through the post. I'm never
going to complain about receiving free early copies of books,
because quite clearly there's nothing to complain about, but it does
introduce a rogue element into one's otherwise carefully plotted
reading schedule. I had no idea I wanted to read Wheen's book
until it arrived, and it was because of Wheen that I read Lewis, and
then *Not Even Wrong* turned up and I wanted to read that too, and
Buchan's *Greenmantle* got put to one side, I suspect forever. Being
a reader is sort of like being president, except reading involves
fewer state dinners, usually. You have this agenda you want to get
through, but you get distracted by life events, e.g., books arriving
in the mail/ World War III, and you are temporarily deflected from
your chosen path.

Having said that I hardly ever read books about autism, I have
now read two in the last few weeks. Paul Collins, occasionally of
this parish, is another parent of an autistic kid, and *Not Even Wrong,*
like Charlotte Moore's *George and Sam,* is a memoir of sorts. The
two books are complementary, though; while writing unsenti-
mentally but movingly about his son Morgan's diagnosis and the
family's response, Collins trawls around, as is his wont, for histori-
cal and contemporary illustration and resonance, and finds plenty.
There's Peter the Wild Boy, who became part of the royal household in the early eighteenth century, and who met Pope, Addison,
Steele, Swift, and Defoe—he almost certainly played for our team.
(Autistic United? Maybe Autistic Wanderers is better.) And Collins
finds a lot of familiar traits among railway-timetable collectors, and
Microsoft boffins, and outsider artists... I'm happy that we're liv-

ing through these times of exceptionally written and imaginative memoirs, despite the incessant whine you hear from the books-pages; Collins's engaging, discursive book isn't as raw as some, but in place of rawness there is thoughtfulness, and thoughtfulness is never a bad thing. I even learned stuff, and you can't often say that of a memoir.

New Year, New Me, another quick read of Gillian Riley's *How to Stop Smoking and Stay Stopped for Good*. I have now come to think of Riley as our leading cessation theorist; she's brilliant, but now I need someone who deals with the practicalities. ✶

APRIL 2004

Last month I was banging on about how books were better than anything—how just about any decent book you picked would beat up anything else, any film or painting or piece of music you cared to match it up with. Anyway, like most theories advanced in this column, it turned out to be utter rubbish. I read four really good books this month, but even so, my cultural highlights of the last four weeks were not literary. I went to a couple of terrific exhibitions at the Royal Academy (and that's a hole in my argument right there—one book might beat up one painting, but what chance has one book, or even four books, got against the collected works of Guston and Vuillard?); I saw Jose Antonio Reyes score his first goal for Arsenal against Chelsea, a thirty-yard screamer, right in the top corner; and someone sent me a superlative Springsteen bootleg, a '75 show at the Main Point in Bryn Mawr with strings, and a cover of "I Want You," and I don't know what else. Like I said, I loved the books that I read this month, but when that Reyes shot hit the back of the net, I was four feet in the air. (The Polysyllabic Spree hates sport, especially soccer, because it requires people to expose their arms and legs, and the Spree believes that all body parts must be covered at all times. So even though I'm not allowed to talk about Reyes at any length, he does look to be some player.) Anyway, Patrick Hamilton didn't even get me to move my feet. I just sat there—lay there, most of the time—throughout the whole thing. So there we are, then. Books: pretty good, but not as good as other stuff, like goals, or bootlegs.

I spent a long time resisting *The Curious Incident of the Dog in the Night-Time* because I got sent about fifteen copies, by publishers and agents and magazines and newspapers, and it made me recalcitrant and reluctant, truculent, maybe even perverse. I got sent fifteen copies because the narrator of *The Curious Incident* has Asperger's syndrome, which places him on the autistic spectrum, although way over the other side from my son. I can see why publishers do this, but the books that arrive in the post tend to be a distorted and somewhat unappetizing version of one's life and work. And what one wants to read, most of the time, is something that bears no reference to one's life and work.

(Twice this week I have been sent manuscripts of books that remind their editors, according to their covering letters, of my writing. Like a lot of writers, I can't really stand my own writing, in the same way that I don't really like my own cooking. And, just as when I go out to eat, I tend not to order my signature dish—an overcooked and overspiced meat-stewy thing containing something inappropriate, like tinned peaches, and a side order of undercooked and flavorless vegetables—I really don't want to read anything that I could have come up with at my own computer. What I produce on my computer invariably turns out to be an equivalent of the under-cooked overcooked stewy thing, no matter how hard I try to follow the recipe, and you really don't want to eat too much of that. I'd love to be sent a book with an accompanying letter that said, "This is nothing like your work. But as a man of taste and discernment, we think you'll love it anyway." That never happens.)

Anyway, I finally succumbed to Mark Haddon's book, simply because it had been recommended to me so many times as a piece of fiction, rather than as a recognizable portrait of my home life. It's the third book about autism I've read in three months, and each book—this one, Charlotte Moore's *George and Sam,* and Paul Collins's *Not Even Wrong*—contains a description of the classic test devised to demonstrate the lack of a theory of mind in autistic children. I'll quote Paul Collins's succinct summary:

> Sally and Anne have a box and a basket in front of them. Sally puts a marble in the basket. Then she leaves the room. While Sally is gone, Anne takes the marble out of the basket and puts it in the box. When Sally comes back in, where will she look for her marble?

If you ask ordinary kids, even ordinary three-year-olds, to observe Sally and Anne and then answer the question, they'll tell you that Sally will look in the basket. An autistic kid, however, will always tell you that Sally should look in the box, because an autis-tic kid is unable to imagine that someone else knows (or feels, or thinks) anything different from himself. In *The Curious Incident,* Christopher attempts to solve a murder-mystery, and one would imagine that of all the career-paths closed off to autists, the path leading to a desk at the FBI is probably the least accessible. If you are profoundly unable to put yourself in someone else's shoes, then a job involving intuition and empathy, second-guessing and psychology is probably not the job for you. Haddon has Christopher, his narrator, refer to the theory-of-mind experiment, and it's the one moment in the book where the author nearly brings his otherwise smartly imagined world crashing about his and our ears. Christopher talks about his own failure in the test, and then says, "That was because when I was little I didn't understand about other people having minds. And Julie said to Mother and Father that I would always find this very difficult. Because I decided it was a kind of puzzle, and if something is a puzzle there is always a way of solving it."

"I decided it was a kind of puzzle..." Hold on a moment: that means—what?—that every Asperger's kid could do this, if they so chose? That the most debilitating part of the condition—effectively, the condition itself—could be removed by an application of will? This is dangerous territory, and I'm not sure Haddon crosses it with absolute conviction. *The Curious Incident* is an absorbing, entertaining, moving book, but when truth gets bent out of shape in this way in order to serve the purposes of a narrative, then maybe it's a book that can't properly be described as a work of art? I don't know. I'm just asking the question. Happily, the detective element of the novel has been pretty much forgotten by the second half, and one description—of Christopher trying and failing to get on a crowded tube train, and then another, and then another, until hours and hours pass—is unforgettable, and very, very real.

In an online interview, Haddon quotes one of his Amazon reviewers, someone who hated his novel, saying, "the most worrying thing about the book is that Christopher says he dislikes fiction, and yet the whole book is fiction." And that, says the author, "puts at least part of the problem in a nutshell." It doesn't, I don't think, because the Amazon reviewer is too dim to put anything in a nutshell. I suspect, in fact, that the Amazon reviewer couldn't put anything in the boot of his car, let alone a nutshell. (Presumably you couldn't write a book about someone who couldn't read, either, or someone who didn't like paper, because the whole book is paper. Oh, man, I hate Amazon reviewers. Even the nice ones, who say nice things. They're bastards too.) But Haddon is right if what he's saying is that picking through a book of this kind for inconsistencies is a mug's game, and I'm sorry if that's what I've done. The part that made me wince a little seemed more funda-mental than an inconsistency, though.

This comes up again in Patrick Hamilton's brilliant *Hangover Square,* where the central character suffers from some kind of schiz-ophrenia. At periodic intervals he kind of blacks out, even though he remains conscious throughout the attacks. ("It was as though a shutter had fallen"; "as though one had blown one's nose too hard and the outer world had become suddenly dim"; "as though he had been watching a talking film, and all at once the sound-track had failed"—because George Bone cannot properly recall the last attack, he searches for fresh ways to describe each new one.) And of course it doesn't quite make sense, because he doesn't know what he's doing when the attacks occur, except he does, really; and he doesn't know who anyone is anymore, except he manages to retain just enough information to make Hamilton's plot work. And it really doesn't matter, because this book isn't about schizophrenia. It's about an exhausted city on the brink of war—it's set in London at the beginning of 1939—and about shiftless drunken fuckups, and it feels astonishingly contemporary and fresh. You may remem-ber that I wanted to read Hamilton because my current favorite rock-and-roll band is naming an album after one of his books, and if that seems like a piss-poor (and laughably unliterary) reason to dig out a neglected minor classic, well, I'm sorry. But I got there in the end, and I'm glad I did. Thank you, Marah. Oh, and George Bone in schizophrenic mode has a hilarious and unfathomable obsession with a town called Maidenhead, which is where I grew up, and which has been for the most part overlooked, and wisely so, throughout the entire history of the English novel. Bone thinks that when he gets to Maidenhead, everything's going to be all right. Good luck with that, George!

I bought Mark Salzman's *True Notebooks* a couple of months ago, after an interview with the author in the *Believer*. I am beginning belatedly to realize that discovering books through reading about them in the *Believer*, and then writing about them in the *Believer*—as I have done once or twice before—is a circular process that doesn't do you any favors. You'd probably like to read about a book you didn't read about a while back. Anyway, as the interview implied, this is a pretty great book, but, *boy* is it sad.

True Notebooks is about Mark Salzman's gig teaching writing at Central Juvenile Hall in L.A., where just about every kid is awaiting trial on a gang-related murder charge. Salzman's just the right person to attempt a book of this kind. He's empathetic and compassionate and all that jazz, but he's no bleeding-heart liberal. At the beginning of the book, he lists all the reasons why he shouldn't get involved in this kind of thing. They include "Students all gang-bangers," "Still angry about getting mugged in 1978," and, even less ambiguously, "Wish we could tilt L.A. County and shake it until everybody with a shaved head and tattoos falls into the ocean." Toward the end of the book, he attends the trial of the student he loves the most, listens to all the extenuating circumstances, and finds himself going to bed that night with a broken heart, just as he feared he would. However, his sadness is engendered "not because of what the legal system was doing to young people… I had to wrap my mind around the fact that someone I had grown so fond of, and who seemed so gentle, had been foolish enough to go to a movie theater carrying a loaded gun, violent enough to shoot three people with it—two of them in the back—and then callous enough to want to go to a movie afterwards."

I don't want to give the impression that *True Notebooks* is unreadable in its gray-grimness, or unpalatably preachy. It's consistently entertaining, and occasionally bleakly funny. "'How about describing a time you helped someone?'" Salzman suggests to a student who is struggling for a topic to write about.

"Mm… I never did anything that nice for anybody."

"It can be a small thing."

"Mm… it's gonna have to be real small, Mark."

This is one of those books where the characters learn and grow and change, and we've all read countless novels and seen countless films like that, and we know what to expect: redemption, right? But *True Notebooks* is real, so the characters learn and grow and change, and then get sentenced to thirty-plus years in prison, where God knows what fate awaits them. In the acknowledgments at the end of the book, Salzman thanks the students for making him decide to have children of his own. It might not be much when set against the suffering and pain both caused and experienced by the kids he teaches, but it's all we've got to work with, and I'm disproportionately glad he mentioned it: when I'd finished *True Notebooks,* Salzman's kids were all I had to keep me going. I'm enjoying *The Long Firm,* Jake Arnott's clever and vivid novel about London's gangland in the 1960s, but I think perhaps *True Notebooks* spoiled it for me a little. Gangland, gangs, guns, murder… none of it is as much fun as you might think.

Next month I'm going to read *David Copperfield,* the only major Dickens I haven't done yet. I'll probably still be reading it the month after, too, so if you want to take a break from this column, now would probably be the time to do it. I've been putting it off for a while, mostly because of the need to read loads of stuff that I can use to fill up these pages, but I'm really feeling the need for a bit of Dickensian nutrition. I don't know what I'll find to say about it, though, and I'm really hoping that Jose Antonio Reyes can help me out of a hole. Are thirty-yard thunderbolts better than Dickens at his best? I'll bet you can't wait to find out. ✲

MAY 2004

Anyone and everyone taking a writing class knows that the secret of good writing is to cut it back, pare it down, winnow, chop, hack, prune and trim, remove every superfluous word, compress, compress, compress. What's that chinking noise? It's the sound of the assiduous creative-writing student hitting bone. You can't read a review of, say, a Coetzee book without coming across the word "spare," used invariably with approval; I just Googled "J. M. Coetzee + spare" and got 907 hits, almost all of them different. "Coetzee's spare but multi-layered language," "detached in

tone and spare in style," "layer upon layer of spare, exquisite sentences," "Coetzee's great gift—and it is a gift he extends to us—is
in his spare and yet beautiful language," "spare and powerful language," "a chilling, spare book," "paradoxically both spare and
richly textured," "spare, steely beauty." Get it? Spare is good.

Coetzee, of course, is a great novelist, so I don't think it's
snarky to point out that he's not the funniest writer in the world.
Actually, when you think about it, not many novels in the Spare
tradition are terribly cheerful. Jokes you can usually pluck out
whole, by the roots, so if you're doing some heavy-duty prose-
weeding, they're the first things to go. And there's some stuff about
the whole winnowing process that I just don't get. Why does it
always stop when the work in question has been reduced to sixty
or seventy thousand words—entirely coincidentally, I'm sure, the
minimum length for a publishable novel? I'm sure you could get
it down to twenty or thirty, if you tried hard enough. In fact, why
stop at twenty or thirty? Why write at all? Why not just jot the plot
and a couple of themes down on the back of an envelope and
leave it at that? The truth is, there's nothing very utilitarian about
fiction or its creation, and I suspect that people are desperate to
make it sound like manly, back-breaking labor because it's such a
wussy thing to do in the first place. The obsession with austerity is
an attempt to compensate, to make writing resemble a real job, like
farming, or logging. (It's also why people who work in advertising
put in twenty-hour days.) Go on, young writers—treat yourself to
a joke, or an adverb! Spoil yourself! Readers won't mind! Have
you ever looked at the size of books in an airport bookstall? The
truth is that people like superfluity. (And, conversely, the writers'
writers, the pruners and the winnowers, tend to have to live off
critical approval rather than royalty checks.)

Last month, I ended by saying that I was in need of some
Dickensian nutrition, and maybe it's because I've been sucking on
the bones of pared-down writing for too long. Where would

David Copperfield be if Dickens had gone to writing classes? Probably about seventy minor characters short, is where. (Did you know that Dickens is estimated to have invented thirteen thousand characters? Thirteen thousand! The population of a small town! If you want to talk about books in terms of back-breaking labor, then maybe we should think about how hard it is to write a lot— long books, teeming with exuberance and energy and life and comedy. I'm sorry if that seems obvious, but it can't always be true that writing a couple of hundred pages is harder than writing a thousand.) At one point near the beginning of the book, David runs away, and ends up having to sell the clothes he's wearing for food and drink. It would be enough, maybe, to describe the physical hardship that ensued; but Dickens being Dickens, he finds a bit part for a real rogue of a secondhand clothes merchant, a really scary guy who smells of rum and who shouts things like "Oh, my lungs and liver" and "Goroo!" a lot.

As King Lear said—possibly when invited in to Iowa as a visiting speaker—"Reason not the need." There is no *need*: Dickens is having fun, and he extends the scene way beyond its function. Rereading it now, it seems almost to have been conceived as a retort to spareness, because the scary guy insists on paying David for his jacket in halfpenny installments over the course of an afternoon, and thus ends up sticking around for two whole pages. Could he have been cut? Absolutely he could have been cut. But there comes a point in the writing process when a novelist—any novelist, even a great one—has to accept that what he is doing is keeping one end of a book away from the other, filling up pages, in the hope that these pages will move, provoke, and entertain a reader.

Some random observations:

1) *David Copperfield* is Dickens's *Hamlet. Hamlet* is a play full of famous quotes; *Copperfield* is a novel full of famous char-

acters. I hadn't read it before, partly because I was under the curious misapprehension that I could remember a BBC serialization that I was forced to watch when I was a child, and therefore would be robbed of the pleasures of the narrative. (It turns out that all I could remember was the phrase "Barkis is willing," and Barkis's willingness isn't really the book's point.) So I really had no idea that I was going to run into both Uriah Heep and Mr. Micawber, as well as Peggotty, Steerforth, Betsey Trotwood, Little Em'ly, Tommy Traddles, and the rest. I'd presumed Dickens would keep at least a couple of those back for some of the other novels I haven't read—*The Pickwick Papers,* say, or *Barnaby Rudge.* But he's blown it now. That might be an error on his part. We shall see, eventually.

2) Why do people keep trying to make movie or TV adaptations of Dickens novels? In the first issue of the *Believer,* Jonathan Lethem asked us to reimagine the characters in *Dombey and Son* as animals, in order to grasp the essence of these characters, and it's true that only the central characters in a Dickens novel are human. Here's Quilp, in *The Old Curiosity Shop,* terrifying Kit's mother with "many extraordinary annoyances; such as hanging over from the side of the coach at the risk of his life, and staring in with his great goggle eyes...; dodging her in this way from one window to another; getting nimbly down whenever they changed horses and thrusting his head in at the window with a dismal squint..." And here's Uriah Heep: "hardly any eyebrows, and no eyelashes, and eyes of a red-brown, so unsheltered and unshaded, that I remember wondering how he went to sleep... high-shouldered and bony... a long, lank skeleton hand... his nostrils, which were thin and pointed, with sharp dints in them, had a singular and most uncomfortable way of

expanding and contracting themselves; that they seemed to twinkle instead of his eyes, which hardly ever twinkled at all." So who would *you* cast as these two? If the right actors ever existed, I'm betting that they wouldn't be much fun to hang out with on set, what with having no social lives, or girlfriends, or prospects of working in anything else ever, apart from *Copperfield 2: Heep's Revenge*. And once these cartoon gremlins take corporeal form, they lose their point anyway. Memo to studios: a mix of CGI and live action is the only way forward. True, it would be expensive, and true, no one would ever want to pay to watch. But if you wish to do the great man justice—and I'm sure that's all you Hollywood execs think about, just as I'm sure you're all subscribers to the *Believer*—then it's got to be worth a shot.

3) In *The Old Curiosity Shop* I discovered that in the character of Dick Swiveller, Dickens provided P. G. Wodehouse with pretty much the whole of his oeuvre. In *David Copperfield,* David's bosses Spenlow and Jorkins are what must be the earliest fictional representations of good cop/bad cop.

4) I have complained in this column before about how everyone wants to spoil plots of classics for you. OK, I should have read *David Copperfield* before, and therefore deserve to be punished. But even the snootiest critic/publisher/whatever must presumably accept that we must all, at some point, read a book for the first time. I know that the only thing brainy people do with their lives is reread great works of fiction, but surely even James Wood and Harold Bloom read before they reread? (Maybe not. Maybe they've only ever reread, and that's what separates them from us. Hats off to them.) Anyway, the great David Gates gives away two or three major narrative developments in the *very first paragraph*

of his introduction to my Modern Library edition (and I think I'm entitled to read the first paragraph, just to get a little context or biographical detail); I tried to check out the film versions on Amazon, and an Amazon reviewer pointlessly gave away another in a three-line review. That wouldn't have happened if I'd been looking for a Grisham adaptation.

5.) At the end of last year, I was given a first edition *David Copperfield* as a prize, and I had this fantasy that I was going to sit in an armchair and read a few pages of it, and feel the power of the great man enter me at my fingertips. Well, I tried it, and nothing happened. Also, the print was really small, and I was scared of dropping it in the bath, absentmindedly putting a cigarette out on it, etc. I actually ended up reading four different copies of the book. An old college Penguin edition fell apart in my hands, so I bought a Modern Library edition to replace it. Then I lost the Modern Library copy, temporarily, and bought another cheap Penguin to replace it. It cost £1.50! That's only about ninety dollars! (That was my attempt at edgy au courant humor. I won't bother again.)

There was a moment, about a third of the way through, when I thought that *David Copperfield* might become my new favorite Dickens novel—which, seeing as I believe that Dickens is the greatest novelist who ever lived, would mean that I might be in the middle of the best book I'd ever read. That superlative way of thinking ceases to become very compelling as you get older, so the realization wasn't as electrifying as you might think. I could see the logic, in the same way that you can see the logic of those ontological arguments that the old philosophers used to trot out to prove that God exists: Dickens = best writer, DC = his best book, therefore DC = best book ever written—without feeling it. But, in the end, there was too much wrong. The young women, as usual, are weedy. Bodies start to pile up in uncomfortable proximity—there are four deaths, if you count drippy Dora's bloody dog, which I don't but Dickens does—between pages 714 and 740. And just when you want the book to wrap up, Dickens inserts a pointless and dull chapter about prison reform, twenty pages from the end. (He's against solitary confinement. Too good for 'em.)

What puts *David Copperfield* right up there with *Bleak House* and *Great Expectations,* however, is its sweet nature, and its surprising modernity. There's some metafictional stuff going on, for example: David grows up to be a novelist, and the full title of the book, according to Edgar Johnson's biography (not that I can find any evidence of this anywhere), is *The Personal History, Experience and Observations of David Copperfield the Younger of Blunderstone Rookery, which he never meant to be published on any account.* And there's a point to the metafictional stuff, too. The last refuge of the scoundrel-critic is any version of the sentence, "Ultimately, this book is about fiction itself/this film is about film itself." I have used the sentence myself, back in the days when I reviewed a lot of books, and it's bullshit: invariably all it means is that the film or novel has drawn attention to its own fictional state, which doesn't get us very far, and which is why the critic never tells us exactly what the novel has to say about fiction itself. (Next time you see the sentence, which will probably be some time in the next seven days if you read a lot of reviews, write to the critic and ask for elucidation.)

Anyway, David Copperfield's profession allows him these piercing little moments of regret and nostalgia; there's a lot about memory in this book, and in an autobiographical novel, memory and fiction get all tangled up. Dickens uses the tangle to his advantage, and I can't remember being so moved by one of his novels. The other thing that seems to me different about *David Copperfield* is the sophistication of a couple of the characters and relationships. Dickens isn't the most sophisticated of writers, and when he does attain complexity, it's because subplot is layered upon subplot, and character over character, until he can't help but get something going. But there's a startlingly contemporary admission of marital dissatisfaction in *Copperfield*, for example, an acknowledgment of lack and of an unspecified yearning that you'd associate more with Rabbit Angstrom than with someone who spends half the novel quaffing punch with Mr. Micawber. Dickens eventually takes the Victorian way out of the twentieth-century malaise, but even so... Making notes for this column, I find that I wrote "He's from another planet"; "Was he a Martian?" David Gates asks in the introduction. And to think that some people don't rate him! To think that some people have described him as "the worst writer to plague the English language"! Yeah, well. You can believe them or you can side with Tolstoy, Peter Ackroyd, and David Gates. And me. Your choice.

For the first time since I've been writing this column, the completion of a book has left me feeling bereft: I miss them all. Let's face it: usually you're just happy as hell to have chalked another one up on the board, but this last month I've been living in this hyperreal world, full of memorable, brilliantly eccentric people, and laughs (I hope you know how funny Dickens is), and proper bendy stories you want to follow. I suspect that it'll be difficult to read a pared-down, stripped-back, skin-and-bones novel for a while. ✸

A *selection from*

DAVID COPPERFIELD
by CHARLES DICKENS

✷ ✷ ✷

Into this shop, which was low and small, and which was dark-ened rather than lighted by a little window, overhung with clothes, and was descended into by some steps, I went with a pal-pitating heart; which was not relieved when an ugly old man, with the lower part of his face all covered with a stubbly grey beard, rushed out of a dirty den behind it, and seized me by the hair of my head. He was a dreadful old man to look at, in a filthy flannel waistcoat, and smelling terribly of rum. His bedstead, covered with a tumbled and ragged piece of patchwork, was in the den he had come from, where another little window showed a prospect of more stinging nettles, and a lame donkey.

"Oh, what do you want?" grinned this old man, in a fierce, monotonous whine. "Oh, my eyes and limbs, what do you want? Oh, my lungs and liver, what do you want? Oh, goroo, goroo!"

I was so much dismayed by these words, and particularly by the repetition of the last unknown one, which was a kind of rattle in his throat, that I could make no answer; hereupon the old man, still holding me by the hair, repeated—

"Oh, what do you want? Oh, my eyes and limbs, what do you want? Oh, my lungs and liver, what do you want? Oh, goroo!"—which he screwed out of himself, with an energy that made his eyes start in his head.

"I want to know" I said, trembling, "if you would buy a jacket."

"Oh, let's see the jacket!" cried the old man. "Oh, my heart on fire, show the jacket to us! Oh, my eyes and limbs, bring the jacket out!"

With that he took his trembling hands, which were like the claws of a great bird, out of my hair; and put on a pair of spectacles, not at all ornamental to his inflamed eyes.

"Oh, how much for the jacket?" cried the old man, "no! Oh, my eyes, no! Oh, my limbs, no! Eighteenpence. Goroo!"

Every time he uttered this ejaculation, his eyes seemed in danger of starting out; and every sentence he spoke, he delivered in a sort of tune, always exactly the same, and more like a gust of wind, which begins low, mounts up high, and falls again, then any other comparison I can find for it.

"Well," I said, glad to have closed the bargain, "I'll take eighteenpence."

"Oh, my liver!" cried the old man, throwing the jacket on a shelf. "Get out of the shop! Oh, my eyes and limbs—goroo!— don't ask for money; make it an exchange."

I was never so frightened in my life, before or since; but I told him humbly that I wanted money, and that nothing else was of any use to me, but that I would wait for it, as he desired, outside, and had no wish to hurry him. So I went outside, and sat down in the shade in a corner. And I sat there so many hours, that the shade became sunlight, and the sunlight became shade again, and still I sat there waiting for the money.

There was never such another drunken madman in that line of business, I hope. That he was well known in the neighborhood, and enjoyed the reputation of having sold himself to the devil, I soon understood from the visits he received from the boys, who continually came skirmishing about the shop, shouting that legend, and calling to him to bring out his gold. "You ain't poor, you know, Charley. Rip it open and let's have some!" This, and many offers to lend him a knife for the purpose, exasperated him to such a degree, that the whole day was a succession of rushes on his part, and flights on the part of the boys. Sometimes in his rage he would take me for one of them, and come at me, mouthing as if he were going to tear me in pieces; then, remembering me, just in time, would dive into the shop, and lie upon his bed, as I thought from the sound of his voice, yelling in a frantic way, to his own windy tune, the Death of Nelson; with an Oh! before every line, and innumerable Goroos interspersed. As if this were not bad enough for me, the boys, connecting me with the establishment, on account of the patience and perseverance with which I sat outside, half-dressed, pelted me, and used me very ill all day.

He made many attempts to induce me to consent to an exchange; at one time coming out with a fishing-rod, at another with a fiddle, at another with a cocked hat, at another with a flute. But I resisted him all these overtures, and sat there in desperation; each time asking him, with tears in my eyes, for my money or my jacket. At last he began to pay me in halfpence at a time; and was full two hours getting by easy stages to a shilling.

"Oh, my eyes and limbs!" he cried, peeping hideously out of the shop, after a long pause, "will you go for twopence more?"

"I can't," I said, "I shall be starved."

"Oh, my lungs and liver, will you go for threepence?"

"I would go for nothing, if I could,' I said, 'but I want the money badly."

"Oh, go-roo!" (it is really impossible to express how he twisted this ejaculation out of himself, as he peeped round the door-post at me, showing nothing but his crafty old head;) "will you go for fourpence?"

I was so faint and weary that I closed with this offer; and taking the money out of his claw, not without trembling, went away more hungry and thirsty than I had ever been, a little before sunset. But at an expense of threepence I soon refreshed myself completely; and, in being in better spirits then, limped seven miles upon my road. ✷

JUNE 2004

The Polysyllabic Spree—the ninety-nine young and menacingly serene people who run the *Believer*—recently took their regular columnists out for what they promised would be a riotous and orgiastic night on the town. Now, I have to confess that I've never actually seen a copy of this magazine, due to an ongoing dispute with the Spree (I think that as a contributor I should be entitled to a free copy, but they are insisting that I take out a ten-year subscription—does that sound right to you?), so I was completely unaware that there is only one other regular columnist, the Croatian sex lady, and she didn't show. I suspect that she'd been given a tip-off, probably because she's a woman (the Spree hold men responsible for the death of Virginia Woolf) and stayed at home. It shouldn't have made much difference, though, because you can have fun with a hundred people, right?

Wrong. The Spree's idea of a good time was to book tickets for a literary event—a reading given by all the nominees for the National Book Critics' Circle Awards—and sit there for two and a half hours. Actually, that's not quite true: they didn't sit there. Such is their unquenchable passion for the written word that they were too excited to sit. They stood, and they wept, and they hugged each other, and occasionally they even danced—to the poetry recitals, and some of the more up-tempo biography nominees. In England we don't often dance at dances, let alone readings, so I didn't know where to look. Needless to say, drink, drugs, food, and sex played no part in the festivities. But who needs any of that when you've got literature?

I did, however, discover a couple of books as a result of the evening: Tony Hoagland's *What Narcissism Means to Me*, which didn't win the poetry award, and Adrian Nicole LeBlanc's *Random Family*, which didn't win the nonfiction award. I haven't read the books that did win, and therefore cannot comment on the judges' inexplicable decisions, but they must be pretty good, because Hoagland's poems and LeBlanc's study of life in the Bronx were exceptional.

Middle-class people—especially young middle-class people— spend an awful lot of time and energy attempting to familiarize themselves with what's going down on the street. *Random Family* is a one-stop shop: it tells you everything you need to know, and may even stop you from hankering after a gun or a crack habit as a quick way out of the graduate-school ghetto. And yes, I know that all reality is mediated, and so on and so forth, but this book does a pretty good job of convincing you that it knows whereof it speaks.

Random Family is about two women, Coco and Jessica; LeBlanc's story, which took her ten years to write and research, begins when they're in their mid-teens, and follows them through the next couple of decades. Despite the simplicity of the setup, it's not always an easy narrative to follow. If LeBlanc were a novelist, you'd have to observe that she's screwed up by overpopulating her book, but Coco and Jessica and the Bronx don't give her an awful lot of choice, because *Random Family* is partly about overpopulation. Coco and Jessica have so many babies, by so many fathers, and their children have so many half-siblings, that at times it's impossible to keep the names straight. By the time the two women are in their early thirties, they have given birth to Mercedes, Nikki, Nautica, Pearl, LaMonte, Serena, Brittany, Stephany, Michael, and Matthew, by Cesar, Torres, Puma (or maybe Victor), Willy (or maybe Puma), Kodak, Wishman, and Frankie. This is a book awash with sperm (Jessica even manages to conceive twins while in prison, after an affair with a guard), and at one stage I was wondering whether it was medically possible for a man to become pregnant through reading it. I think I'm probably too old.

The combination of LeBlanc's scrupulous attention to quotidian detail and her absolute refusal to judge is weirdly reminiscent of Peter Guralnick's approach to Elvis in his monumental two-volume biography. Those of you who read the Elvis books will know that though Presley's baffling, infuriating last decade gave Guralnick plenty of opportunity to leap in and tell you what he thinks, he never once does so. LeBlanc's stern neutrality is generous and important: she hectors nobody, and the space she leaves us allows us to think properly, to recognize for ourselves all the millions of complications that shape these lives.

There are many, many things, a *zillion* things, that make my experiences different from those of Coco and Jessica. But it was remembering my first pregnancy scare that helped me to fully understand the stupidity and purposelessness of the usual conservative rants about responsibility and fecklessness and blah blah blah. It was the summer before I went to college, and my girl-friend's period was late, and I spent two utterly miserable weeks convinced that my life was over. I'd have to get, like, an office job, and I'd miss out on three years pissing around at university, and my brilliant career as a... as a something or other would be over before it had even begun. We'd used birth control, of course, because failing to do so would cost us everything, including a very great deal of money, but we were still terrified: I would just as soon have gone to prison as started a family. What *Random Family* explains, movingly and convincingly and at necessary length, is that the future as Coco and Jessica and the fathers of their children see it really isn't worth the price of a condom, and they're right. I eventually became a father for the first time around the same age that Jessica became a grandmother.

As I hadn't noticed the publication of *Random Family*, I caught up with the reviews online. They were for the most part terrific, although one or two people wondered aloud whether LeBlanc's presence might not have affected behavior and outcome. (Yeah, right. I can see how that might work for an afternoon, but a whole decade? Stick a writer in a corner of the room and watch the combined forces of international economics, the criminal justice system, and the drug trade wither before her pitiless gaze.) "I believe I had far less effect than anybody would imagine," LeBlanc said in an interview, with what I like to imagine as wry understatement. I did come across this, however, the extraordinary conclusion to a review in the *Guardian* (U.K.):

> It is only by accident, in the acknowledgements, that the book finally confronts the reader with the "American experience of class injustice" that is ostensibly its subject. So many institutions, so many funds and fellowships, retreat centers and universities, pub-lishers, mentors, editors, friends, formed a net to support this one

writer. Nothing comparable exists to hold up the countless Cocos and Jessicas...

But the tougher question is why the stories of poor people—and not just any poor people but those acquainted with chaos and crime, those the overclass likes to call the underclass—are such valuable raw material, creating a frisson among the literary set and the buyers of books? Why are their lives and private griefs currency for just about anyone but themselves?

First of all: "by accident"? "BY ACCIDENT"? Those two words, so coolly patronizing and yet, paradoxically, so dim, must have made LeBlanc want to buy a gun. And I think a decent lawyer could have gotten her off, in the unfortunate event of a shooting. She spends ten years writing a book, and a reviewer in a national newspaper doesn't even notice what it's about. (It's about the American experience of class injustice, among other things.) Second: presumably the extension of the argument about grants and fellowships and editors is that they are only appropriate for biographies of bloody, I don't know, Vanessa Bell; I doubt whether "the support net" has ever been put to better social use.

And last: if you get to the end of *Random Family* and conclude that it was written to create "a frisson," then, I'm sorry, but you should be compelled to have your literacy surgically removed, without anesthetic. The lives of Coco and Jessica are "valuable raw material" because people who read books—quite often people who are very quick to judge, quite often people who make or influence social policy—don't know anyone like them, and certainly have no idea how or sometimes even why they live; until we all begin to comprehend, then nothing can even begin to change. Oh, and there's no evidence to suggest that Coco and Jessica resented being used in this way; there is plenty of evidence to suggest that they got it. But what would they know, right?

It's not humorless, either, although of necessity the humor

tends to be a little bleak. When Coco is asked, as part of her application, for an essay entitled "Why I Want to Live in Public
Housing," she writes simply, "Because I'm homeless." And a
description of the office Christmas party thrown by Jessica's
major-duty drug-dealing boyfriend Boy George is hilarious, if
you're able to laugh at the magnitude of your misapprehensions
concerning the wages of sin. (The party took place on a yacht.
There were 121 guests, who ate steak tartare and drank twelve
grand's worth of Moët, and who won Hawaiian trips and
Mitsubishis in the raffle. The Jungle Brothers, Loose Touch, and
Big Daddy Kane performed. Are you listening, Spree?)

George is banged up in the end, of course, so mostly Jessica
and Coco are eating rice and beans, when they're eating at all, and
moving from one rat-infested dump to the next. Luckily we don't
have poverty in England, because Tony Blair eradicated it shortly
after he came to power in 1997. (Note to *Guardian* reviewer—that
was a joke.) But American people should really read this book.
That's "should" as in, It's really good, and "should" as in, You're a
bad person if you don't.

I warned you that this was going to be a nonfiction month.
I started three novels, all of them warmly recommended by friends
or newspapers, and I came to the rather brilliant conclusion that
not one of them was *David Copperfield,* the last novel I read, and
the completion of which has left a devastating hole in my life. So
it seemed like a good time to find out about Coco and Jessica and
Bobby Fischer, real people I knew nothing about. *Bobby Fischer
Goes to War* isn't the most elegantly written book I've ever read,
but the story it tells is so compelling—so hilarious, so nutty, so resonant—that you forgive it its prose trespasses.

When Fischer played Spassky in Reykjavik in 1972 I was fifteen, and not yet worrying about whether anyone was pregnant.
You heard about chess all the time that summer, on the TV and on
the radio, and I presumed that you always heard about chess in the

year of a World Chess Championship, that I'd simply been too young to notice the previous tournament. That happened all the time when you were in your early teens: things that only rolled around every few years, like elections and Olympics, suddenly assumed a magnitude you'd never known they possessed, simply because you were more media-aware. The truth in this case was, of course, that no one had ever talked about chess before, and no one ever would again, really. Everyone was talking about Fischer: Fischer and his refusal to play, Fischer and his demands for more money (he just about bankrupted an entire country by demanding a bigger and bigger chunk of the purse, and then refusing to allow the Icelanders to recoup it through TV and film coverage), Fischer and his forfeit of the second game, Fischer and his absence from the opening ceremony... You could make an absolutely gripping film of Reykjavik '72 that would end with the very first move of the very first match, and that would be about pretty much everything.

Tony Hoagland is the sort of poet you dream of finding but almost never do. His work is relaxed, deceptively easy on the eye and ear, and it has jokes and unexpected little bursts of melancholic resonance. Plus, I pretty much understand all of it, and yet it's clever—as you almost certainly know, contemporary poetry is a kind of Reykjavik, a place where accessibility and intelligence have been fighting a Cold War by proxy for the last half-century. If something doesn't give you even a shot at comprehension in the first couple of readings, then my motto is "Fuck it," but I never swore once. They can use that as a blurb, if they want. They should. Who wouldn't buy a poetry book that said "I never swore once" on the cover? Everyone would know what it meant. And isn't *What Narcissism Means to Me* a great title?

I cheated a little with *What Narcissism Means to Me*—I read it last month, immediately after my night on the town with the Spree. But I wanted this clean *Copperfield* line in my last column, and anyway I was worried that I'd be short of stuff this month, not least because it's been a big football month. Arsenal lost the Champions League quarterfinal to Chelsea, lost the FA Cup semi to Man Utd., and then, just this last weekend, won the Championship. (The two losses were in knock-out competitions. The Championship is what counts, really. That's what we're all telling ourselves here in Highbury.) So on Sunday night, when I should have been reading stuff, I was in a pub called the Bailey, as has become traditional on Championship nights, standing on a chair and singing a comical song about Victoria Beckham. To be honest, I thought if I threw in some poetry, you might like me more. I thought I might even like myself more. Anyway, the standing on the chair and singing wasn't as much fun as the consumption of contemporary literature, obviously, but, you know. It was still pretty good. ✶

IMPOSSIBLE DREAM

by TONY HOAGLAND

✫ ✫ ✫

In Delaware a congressman
      accused of sexual misconduct
says clearly at the press conference
      speaking
           right into the microphone
that he would like very much
          to do it again.

It was on the radio
      and Carla laughed
as she painted, *Die, You Pig*
        in red nail polish
on the back of a turtle
she plans to turn loose tomorrow
        in Jerry's backyard

We lived near the high school that year
and in the afternoons, in autumn,
you could hear the marching-band rehearsals
from the stadium:
      off-key trumpets smeared and carried by the wind,
drums and weirdly-bent trombones:

a ragged "Louie Louie"
      or sometimes, "The Impossible Dream."
I was reading a book about pleasure,
how you have to glide through it
      without clinging,
like an arrow,

passing through a target,
                coming out the other side and going on.

Sitting at the picnic table
carved with the initials of the previous tenants;
                thin October sunlight
blessing the pale grass—
you would have said we had it all—

But the turtle in Carla's hand
churned its odd, stiff legs like oars,
as if it wasn't made for holding still,

and the high-school band played
                worse than ever for a moment
as if getting the song right
                was the impossible dream.

JULY 2004

If you wanted to draw a family tree of everything I read and bought this month—and you never know, it could be fun, if you're a writer, say, or a student, and there are several large holes in your day—you'd have to put *McSweeney's* 13 and Pete Dexter's novel *Train* right at the top.[2] They're the Adam and Eve here, or

---

[1] I bought so many books this month it's obscene, and I'm not owning up to them all: this is a selection. And to be honest, I've been economical with the truth for months now. I keep finding books that I bought, didn't read, and didn't list.

[2] [We do indeed pay Nick Hornby to write his monthly column, but we didn't pay him to mention *McSweeney's* 13.—Ed.]

they would be if Adam and Eve had been hermaphrodites, each able to give birth independently of the other. *McSweeney's* 13 and *Train* never actually mated to produce a beautiful synthesis of the two; and nor did any of the other books actually get together, either. So it would be a pretty linear family tree, to be honest: one straight line coming out of *McSweeney's* 13, because *McSweeney's* begat a bunch of graphic novels (*McSweeney's* 13, edited by Chris Ware, is a comics issue, if you're not from 'round these parts), and another straight line coming out of *Train,* which leads to a bunch of nonfiction books, for reasons I will come to later. *Train* didn't directly beget anything, although it did plant some seeds. (I know what you're thinking. You're thinking, Well, if *Train* and *McSweeney's* 13 never actually mated, and if *Train* never directly begat anything, then how good is this whole family-tree thing? And my answer is, Oh, it's good. Trust me. I have a writer's instinct.) Anyway, if you do decide to draw the family tree, the good news is that it's easy; the bad news is that it's boring, point-less, and arguably makes no sense. Up to you.

Pete Dexter's *Train* was carefully chosen to reintroduce me to the world of fiction, a world I have been frightened of visiting ever since I finished *David Copperfield* a couple of months back. I've read Dexter before—*The Paperboy* is a terrific novel—and the first couple of chapters of *Train* are engrossing, complicated, fresh, and real, and I really thought I was back on the fictional horse. But then, in the third chapter, there is an episode of horrific violence, graphically rendered, and suddenly I was no longer under the skin of the book, the way I had been; I was on the outside looking in. What happens is that in the process of being raped, the central female character gets her nipple sliced off, and it really upset me. I mean, I know I was supposed to get upset. But I was bothered way beyond function. I was bothered to the extent that I struck up a conversation with the author at periodic intervals thereafter. "Did the nipple really have to go, Pete? Explain to me why.

Couldn't it have just... nearly gone? Or maybe you could have left it alone altogether? I mean, come on, man. Her husband has just been brutally murdered. She's been raped. We get the picture. Leave the nipple alone."

I am, I think, a relatively passive reader, when it comes to fiction. If a novelist tells me that something happened, then I tend to believe him, as a rule. In his memoir *Experience,* Martin Amis recalls his father, Kingsley, saying that he found Virginia Woolf's fictional world "wholly contrived: when reading her he found that he kept interpolating hostile negatives, murmuring 'Oh no she didn't' or 'Oh no he hadn't' or 'Oh no it wasn't' after each and every authorial proposition"; I only do that when I'm reading something laughably bad (although after reading that passage in *Experience,* I remember it took me a while to shake off Kingsley's approach to the novel). But in the nipple-slicing incident in *Train,* I thought I could detect Dexter's thumb on the scale, to use a brilliant Martin Amis phrase from elsewhere in *Experience.* It seemed to me as though poor Norah lost her nipple through a worldview rather than through a narrative inevitability; and despite all the great storytelling and the muscular, grave prose, and the richness and resonance of the setup (Train is a golf caddy in 1950s L.A., and the novel is mostly about race) I just sort of lost my grip on the book. Also, someone gets shot dead at the end, and I wasn't altogether sure why. That's a sure sign that you haven't been paying the right kind of attention. It should always be clear why someone gets shot. If I ever shoot you, I promise you there will be a really good explanation, one you will grasp immediately, should you live.

While I was in the middle of *Train,* I went browsing in a remainder bookshop, and came across a copy of Frank Kermode's memoir *Not Entitled.* I knew of Kermode's work as a critic, but I didn't know he'd written a memoir, some of which is about his childhood on the Isle of Man, and when I saw it, I was seized by a need to own it. This need was entirely created by poor Norah in *Train*. There would be no nipple-slicing in *Not Entitled*, I was sure of it. I even started to read the thing in a cab on the way home, and although I gave up pretty quickly (it probably went too far the other way—it's a delicate balance I'm trying to strike here), it was very restorative.

I bought Claire Tomalin's gripping, informative *The Invisible Woman* at the Dickens Museum in Doughty Street, London, which is full of all sorts of cool stuff: marked-up reading copies that say things like "SIGH here," letters, the original partwork editions of the novels, and so on. The thing is, I really want to read a Dickens biography, but they're all too long. Ackroyd's is a frankly hilarious 1,140 pages, excluding notes and postscript. (It has a great blurb on the front, the Ackroyd: "An essential book for anyone who has ever loved *or read* Dickens," says P. D. James [my italics]. Can you imagine? You flog your way through *Great Expectations* at school, hate it, and then find you've got to read a thousand pages of biography! What a pisser!) So both the museum visit and the Tomalin book—about his affair with the actress Nelly Ternan—were my ways of fulfilling a need to find out more about the great man without killing myself.

Here's something I found out in *The Invisible Woman*: the son of Charles Dickens's mistress died during my lifetime. He wasn't Dickens's son, but even so: I could have met a guy who said, "Hey, my mum slept with Dickens." I wouldn't have understood what he meant, because I was only two, and as Tomalin makes clear, he wouldn't have wanted to own up anyway, because he was traumatized by what he found out about his mother's past. It's still weird, though, I think, to see how decades—centuries—can be eaten up like that.

Ackroyd, by the way, disputes that Ternan and Dickens ever had an affair. He concedes that Chas set her up in a couple of houses, one in France, and disappeared for long stretches of time in order to visit her, but he won't accept that Dickens was an adulterer: that sort of explanation might work for an ordinary man, he says, but Dickens "was not 'ordinary' in any sense." *The Invisible Woman* is such a formidable work of scholarship, however, that it leaves very little room for doubt. Indeed, Claire Tomalin is so consumed by her research, so much the biographer, that she actually takes Dickens to task for destroying evidence of his relationship with Nelly Ternan. "Dickens himself would not have welcomed our curiosity," she says. "He would have been happier to have every letter he ever wrote dealt with as Nelly... dealt with the bundles of twelve years' intimate correspondence. [She destroyed it all.] He was wrong by any standards."

Don't you love that last sentence? The message is clear: if you're a writer whose work will interest future generations, and you're screwing around, don't delete those emails because Claire Tomalin and her colleagues are going to need them. Zadie Smith and Michael Chabon and the rest of you, watch out. (I'm not implying, of course, that either of you is screwing around, and I'm sorry if you made that inference. It was supposed to be a compliment. It just came out wrong. Forget it, OK? And sue the Spree, not me. It was their sloppy editing.)

This Is Serbia Calling, Matthew Collin's book about the Belgrade radio station B92 and the role it played in resisting Milosevic, has been lying around my house for a while. But when my post–*McSweeney's* 13 research into comic books led me to conclude that I should buy, among other things, Joe Sacco's *Safe Area Gorazde,* I wanted to do a little extra reading on the Yugoslavian wars, and Collin's book is perfect: it gives you a top-notch potted history, as well as an enthralling and humbling story about very brave young people refusing to be cowed by a brutal regime. It's pretty funny, too, in places. If you have a taste for that hopelessly bleak Eastern European humor, then the Serbian dissenter of the 1990s is your sort of guy. You've got warring nationalist groups, and an inflation rate in January '94 of 313,563,558 percent (that's on the steep side, for those of you with no head for economics) that resulted in a loaf of bread costing 4,000,000,000 dinars. You've got power cuts, rigged elections, a government too busy committing genocide to worry about the niceties of free speech and, eventually, NATO bombs. There are good jokes to be made, by those with the stomach for them. "The one good thing about no electricity," one cynic remarked during the power failures, "is that there's no television telling us we've got electricity." *This Is Serbia Calling* is essential reading if you've ever doubted the power or the value of culture, of music, books, films, theater; it also makes a fantastic case for Sonic Youth and anyone else who makes loud, weird noises. When your world is falling round about your ears, Tina Turner isn't going to do it for you.

Y: The Last Man is a comic-book series about a world run by women, after every man but one has been wiped out by a mysterious plague. It's a great premise, and full of smart ideas: the Democrats are running the country, because the only Republican women are Republican wives; Israel is cleaning up in the Middle East, because they have the highest proportion of trained female combat soldiers. It's strange, reading a comic—a proper comic, not a graphic novel—in which a woman says, "You can fuck my tits if you want" (and I can only apologize, not only for repeating the expression, but for the number of references to breasts in this month's column. I'm pretty sure it's a coincidence, although we should, I suppose, recognize the possibility that it marks the beginning of a pathetic middle-aged obsession). Is that what happens in comics now? Is this the sort of stuff your ten-year-old boy is reading? Crikey. When I was ten, the only word I'd have understood in the whole sentence would have been "you," although not necessarily in this context. Daniel Clowes's *David Boring*—yeah, yeah, late again—is partly about large bottoms, but as one of the reviews quoted on the back called the book "perverse and fetishistic," I'd have wanted my money back if it hadn't been. It's also clever, and the product of a genuinely odd imagination.

There's no rule that says one's reading has to be tonally consistent. I can't help but feel, however, that my reading has been all over the place this month. *The Invisible Woman* and *Y: The Last Man* were opposites in just about every way you can imagine; they even had opposite titles. A woman you can't see versus a guy whose mere existence attracts the world's attention. Does this matter? I suspect it might. I was once asked to DJ at a *New Yorker* party, and the guy who was looking after me (in other words, the guy who was actually playing the records) wouldn't let me choose the music I wanted because he said I wasn't paying enough attention to the beats per minute: according to him, you can't have a differential of more than, I don't know, twenty bpm between records. At the time, I thought this was a stupid idea, but there is a possibility that it might apply to reading. *The Invisible Woman* is pacy and engrossing, but it's no graphic novel, and reading Tomalin's book after *The Last Man* was like playing John Lee Hooker after the Chemical Brothers—in my opinion, John Lee Hooker is the greater artist, but he's in no hurry, is he? Next month, I might try starting with the literary equivalent of a smoocher, and move on to something a bit quicker. And I promise that if there are any breasts, I won't mention them. In fact, I won't even look at them. ✷

AUGUST 2004

S hortly after I submitted my copy for last month's column, my
third son was born. I mention his arrival not because I'm after
your good wishes or your sympathy, but because reading is a
domestic activity, and is therefore susceptible to any changes in the
domestic environment. And though it's true that the baby is
responsible for everything I read this month, just about, he's been
subtle about it: he hasn't made me any more moronic than I was
before, and he certainly hasn't prevented me from reading. He
could argue, in fact, that he has actually encouraged reading in our

household, through his insistence on the increased consciousness of his parents. (Hey—if you lot are all so brainy and so serious about books, how come you're still using contraception?)

Shortly after the birth of a son, I panic that I will never be able to visit a bookshop again, and that therefore any opportunity I have to buy printed matter should be exploited immediately. Jesse (and yes, the T. J. Stiles bio was bought as a tribute) was born shortly before 7 a.m.; three or four hours later I was in a news-agent's, and I saw a small selection of best-selling paperbacks. There wasn't an awful lot there that I wanted, to be honest; but because of the consumer fear, something had to be bought, right there and then, just in case, and I vaguely remembered reading something good about Dennis Lehane's *Mystic River*. Well, the shop didn't have a copy of *Mystic River,* but they did have another Dennis Lehane book, *Prayers for Rain*: that would have to do. Never mind that, as regular readers of this column know, I have over the last few months bought several hundred books I haven't yet read. And never mind that, as it turned out, I found myself passing a book-shop the very next day, and the day after that (because what else is there to do with a new baby, other than mooch around bookshops with him?), and was thus able to buy *Mystic River*. I didn't know for sure I'd ever go to a bookshop again; and if I never went to a bookshop again, how long were those several hundred books going to last me? Nine or ten years at the most. No, I needed that copy of *Prayers for Rain,* just to be on the safe side.

And then, when the baby was a couple of weeks old, I became convinced that I was turning into a vegetable, and so took urgent corrective action: I bought and read, in its entirety, Jonathan Coe's five-hundred page biography of B. S. Johnson, an obscure experi-mental novelist—again, just to be on the safe side, just to prove I still could, even though I never did. I'm hoping that the essential anti-vegetative nutrients and minerals I ingested will last me for a while, that they won't be expelled from the brain via snot or saliva, because I'm not sure when I will next get the chance to read a few hundred pages about a difficult writer I've never read. It almost certainly won't be for a couple of months.

They actually make a very nice theoretical contrast, Johnson and Dennis Lehane. Johnson thought that our need for narrative, our desire to find out what happens next, was "primitive" and "vulgar," and if you took that vulgarity out of *Prayers for Rain,* there wouldn't be an awful lot left. *Prayers for Rain* is "a Kenzie and Gennaro novel," and if I'd spotted those words on the cover, I probably wouldn't have read it. I appreciate that I'm in a minority here, but I just don't get the appeal of the reappearing hero. I don't get Kay Scarpetta, or James Bond, or Hercule Poirot; I don't even get Sherlock Holmes. My problem is that, when I'm reading a novel, I have a need—a childish need, B. S. Johnson would argue—to believe that the events described therein are definitive, that they really matter to the characters. In other words, if 1987 turned out to be a real bitch of a year for Winston Smith, then I don't want to be wasting my time reading about what happened to him back in '84. The least one can ask, really, is that fictional characters should be able to remember the stuff that's happened to them, but I get the impression that Kenzie and Gennaro would struggle to distinguish the psycho killer they're tracking down in *Prayers for Rain* from the psycho killers they've tracked down in other books.

There is a rather dispiriting moment in *Prayers for Rain* that seems to confirm this suspicion. Angie Gennaro, who is involved both professionally and romantically with Patrick Kenzie, asks whether she can shave off his stubble—stubble that he has grown to cover scars. "I considered it," Kenzie tells us. "Three years with protective facial hair. Three years hiding the damage delivered on the worst night of my life…" Hang on a moment. The worst night of your life was *three years ago*? So what am I reading about now? The fourth-worst night of your life? Sometimes, when you walk into a pub in the center of town mid-evening, you get the feeling that you've missed the moment: all the after-work drinkers have gone home, and the late-night drinkers haven't arrived, and there are empty glasses lying around (and the ashtrays are full, if you're drinking in a civilized country), and you didn't make any of the mess... Well, that's kind of how I felt reading *Prayers for Rain*.

I liked Lehane's writing, though. It's humane, and humorous at the right moments, and he has a penchant for quirky cultural references: I hadn't expected a discussion about David Denby's film criticism, for example. (On the other hand: would someone who reads Denby accuse someone who uses the word "finite" of showing off?) I was more than happy to plough straight on into the next one. And the next one was absolutely fantastic.

Why hasn't anyone ever told me that *Mystic River* is right up there with *Presumed Innocent* and *Red Dragon*? Because I don't know the right kind of people, that's why. In the last three weeks, about five different people have told me that Alan Hollinghurst's *The Line of Beauty* is a work of genius, and I'm sure it is; I intend to read it soonest. (Luckily, I happened to be passing a bookshop with the baby, and I was able to pick up a copy.) I'm equally sure, however, that I won't walk into a lamp-post while reading it, like I did with *Presumed Innocent* all those years ago; you don't walk into lamp-posts when you're reading literary novels, do you? How are we supposed to find out about landmark thrillers like *Mystic River*? Anyway, if you haven't seen the movie (and the same goes for *Presumed Innocent* and *Red Dragon*) then take *Mystic River* with you next time you get on a plane, or a holiday, or a toilet, or into a bath, or a bed. Onto or into anything.

Years and years ago, I read a great interview with Jam and Lewis, the R&B producers, in which they described what it was like to be members of Prince's band. They'd sit down, and Prince would tell them what he wanted them to play, and they'd explain that they couldn't—they weren't quick enough, or good enough. And Prince would push them and push them until they mastered it, and then, just when they were feeling pleased with themselves for accomplishing something they didn't know they had the capacity for, he'd tell them the dance steps he needed to accompany the music.

This story has stuck with me, I think, because it seems like an encapsulation of the very best and most exciting kind of creative process, and from the outside, the craft involved in the creation of *Mystic River* looks as though it must have involved the same stretch. Lehane has done everything that a literary novelist is supposed to be able to do (this is a novel about grief, a community, the childhood ties that bind); the intensely satisfying whodunit element is the equivalent of the dance step on top. Indeed, Lehane has ended up making it look so effortless that no one I've ever met seems to have noticed he's done anything much at all. But then, the lesson of literature over the last eighty-odd years is the old math teacher's admonishment: "SHOW YOUR WORKINGS!" Otherwise, how is anyone to know that there are any?

In *Prayers for Rain,* Lehane piles complication upon complication in order to keep his detectives guessing, and there is a certain readerly pleasure to be had from that, of course; but it just seems like a more routine pleasure, compared to what he does in *Mystic River.* There, Lehane peers into the deep, dark hole that the murder of a young girl leaves in various lives, and tries to make sense of everything revealed therein; everything seems organic, nothing—or almost nothing, anyway—feels contrived. I'm happy to have friends who recommend Alan Hollinghurst, really I am. They're all nice, bright people. I just wish I had friends who could recommend books like *Mystic River,* too. Are you that person? Do you have any vacancies for a pal? If you can't be bothered with a full-on friendship, with all the tearful, drunken late-night phone calls and bitter accusations and occasional acts of violence thus entailed (the violence is always immediately followed by an apology, I hasten to add), then maybe you could just tell me the titles of the books.

At the time of writing, *Like a Fiery Elephant,* Jonathan Coe's brilliant biography of B. S. Johnson, doesn't have a U.S. publisher, which seems absurd. Your guys seem to have been frightened off by Johnson's obscurity, but we've never heard of him, either; the book works partly because its author anticipates our ignorance. It also works because Jonathan Coe, probably the best English novelist of his generation (my generation, as bad luck would have it), has been imaginative and interrogative about the form and shape of the book, and because it's a book about writing, perhaps more than anything else. Johnson may have been a 1960s experimentalist who hung out with Beckett and cut holes in his books, but he was as egocentric and arrogant and bitter and money-obsessed as the rest of us. Johnson was a depressive who eventually killed himself; his suicide note read:

This is my last

word.

But he was a great comic character, too, almost Dickensian in his appetites and his propensity for pomposity. Whenever he wrote to complain to publishers, or agents, or even printers—and he complained a lot, not least because he got through a large number of publishers, agents, and printers—he was never backwards in coming forwards, as we say here, and he included the same self-promoting line again and again. "In reviewing my novel *Albert Angelo,* the Sunday *Times* described me as 'one of the best writers we've got,' and the Irish *Times* called the book 'a masterpiece' and put me in the same class as Joyce and Beckett," he wrote to Allen Lane, the founder of Penguin, demanding to know why he wasn't interested in paperback rights. "The Sunday *Times* called me 'one of the best writers we've got,' and the Irish Times called the book a masterpiece and put me in the same class as James Joyce and

Samuel Beckett," he wrote to his foreign rights agent, demanding to know why there had been no Italian publication of his first novel. "You ignorant unliterary Americans make me puke," he wrote to Thomas Wallace of Holt, Rhinehart and Winston, Inc. after Wallace had turned him down. (Maybe Coe should write a version of the same letter, if you ignorant unliterary Americans still refuse to publish his book.) "For your information, *Albert Angelo* was reviewed by the Sunday *Times* here as by 'one of the best writers we've got,' and the Irish *Times* called the book a masterpiece and put me in the same class as Joyce and Beckett." And then, finally and gloriously:

> ...The Sunday *Times* called me 'one of the best writers we've got,' and the Irish *Times* called the book a masterpiece, and compared me with Joyce and Beckett.
>
> However, it seems that I am to be denied the opportunity of a most profound and enormous experience: of being present with my wife Virginia when our first child is born at your hospital on or about July 24th...

This last letter was to the Chief Obstetrician of St. Bartholomew's Hospital in London, after Johnson had discovered that it was not the hospital's policy to allow fathers to attend a birth. It's the "However" kicking off the second paragraph that's such a brilliant touch, drawing attention as it does to the absurdity of the contradiction. "I can understand you keeping out the riff-raff, your Flemings and your Amises and the rest of the what-happened-next brigade," it implies. "But surely you'll make an exception for a genius?" In the end, it's just another variation on "Don't you know who I am?"—which in Johnson's case was an even more unfortunate question than it normally is. Nobody knew then, and nobody knows now.

Johnson had nothing but contempt for the enduring influence of Dickens and the Victorian novel; strange, then, that in the end he should remind one of nobody so much as the utilitarian school inspector in the opening scene of *Hard Times*. Here's the school inspector: "I'll explain to you… why you wouldn't paper a room with representations of horses. Do you ever see horses walking up and down the sides of rooms in reality—in fact?… Why, then, you are not to see anywhere what you don't see in fact; you are not to have anywhere what you don't have in fact. What is called Taste is only another name for Fact." And here's Johnson: "Life does not tell stories. Life is chaotic, fluid, random; it leaves myriads of ends untied, untidily. Writers can extract a story from life only by strict, close selection, and this must mean falsification. Telling stories really is telling lies." Like communists and fascists, Johnson and the dismal inspector wander off in opposite directions, only to discover that the world is round. I'm glad that they both lost the cultural Cold War: there's room for them all in our world, but there's no room for *Mystic River* in theirs. And what kind of world would that be? ✶

SEPTEMBER 2004

Twelve months! A whole year! I don't think I've ever held down a job for this long. And I have to say that when I first met the Polysyllabic Spree, the eighty-four chillingly ecstatic young men and women who run the *Believer*, I really couldn't imagine contributing one column, let alone a dozen. The Spree all live together in Believer Towers, high up in the hills somewhere; they spend their days reading Montaigne's essays aloud to each other (and laughing ostentatiously at the funny bits), shooting at people who own TV sets, and mourning the deaths of every single writer since the Gawain-Poet, in chronological order. When I first met them, they'd got up to Gerard Manley Hopkins. (They seemed particularly cut up about him. It may have been the Jesuit thing, kindred spirits and all that.) I was impressed by their seriousness and their progressive sexual relationships, but they really didn't seem like my kind of people.

And yet here we are, still. I'm beginning to see through the white robes to the people beneath, as it were, and they're really not so bad, once you get past the incense, the vegan food, and the communal showers. They've definitely taught me things: they've taught me, for example, that there is very little point in persisting with a book that isn't working for me, and even less point in writing about it. In snarky old England, we're used to working the other way around—we only finish books that aren't working for us, and those are definitely the only ones we write about. Anyway, as a consequence, my reading has become more focused and less chancy, and I no longer choose novels that I know in advance will make me groan, snort, and guffaw.

I still make mistakes, though, despite the four-hundred-page manual they make you read before you can contribute to the *Believer,* and I made two in the last four weeks. The biography I abandoned was of a major cultural figure of the twentieth century—he died less than forty years ago—so when you see, in the opening chapter, the parentheses "(1782–1860)" after a name, it's really only natural that you become a little disheartened: you're a long, long way from the action. I made it through to the subject's birth, but then got irritated by a long-winded story about a prank he played on a little girl when he was seven. I had always suspected, even before I knew anything about him, that this major cultural figure was once a small boy, so the confirmation was superfluous. And the prank was so banal that he could just as easily have grown up to be Hemingway, or Phil Silvers, or any other midcentury colossus. It wasn't, like, a revealingly or quintessentially _____esque prank. At that point I threw the book down in disgust, and it went straight through the bedroom floor, only just missing a small child. Please, biographers. Please, please, please. Have mercy. Select for us. We have jobs, kids, DVD players, season tickets. But that doesn't mean we don't want to know about stuff.

My other mistake was a literary first novel, and I've probably broken every rule in the Spree manual just by saying that much. I took every precaution, I promise: I was reading a paperback that came garlanded with superlative reviews, and there were a couple of recommendations involved, although I can see now that they came from untrustworthy sources. I ignored the most boring opening sentence I have ever read in my life and ploughed on, prepared to forgive and forget; I got halfway through before its quietness and its lack of truth started to get me down. I don't mind nothing happening in a book, but nothing happening in a phony way—characters saying things people never say, doing jobs that don't fit, the whole works—is simply asking too much of a reader. Something happening in a phony way must beat nothing happening in a phony way every time, right? I mean, you could prove that, mathematically, in an equation, and you can't often apply science to literature.

Here's Tom Shone writing about Spielberg's *Jaws* in his book *Blockbuster*:

> What stays with you, even today, are less the movie's big action moments than the crowning gags, light as air, with which Spielberg gilds his action—Dreyfuss crushing his Styrofoam cup, in response to Quint's crushing of his beercan, or Brody's son copying his finger-steepling at the dinner table...
>
> To get anything resembling such fillets of improvised characterisation, you normally had to watch something far more boring— some chamber piece about marital disintegration by John

Cassavetes, say—and yet here were such things, popping up in a movie starring a scary rubber shark. It was nothing short of revolutionary: you could have finger steepling and scary rubber sharks *in the same movie.* This seemed like important information. Why had no one told us this before?

If this column has anything like an aesthetic, it's there: you can get finger-steepling and sharks in the same book. And you really need the shark part, because a whole novel about finger steepling—and that's a fair synopsis of both the Abandoned Literary Novel and several thousand others like it—can be on the sleepy side. You don't have to have a shark, of course; the shark could be replaced by a plot, or, say, thirty decent jokes.

Tom Shone is a friend, and I've known him for ages—he's younger than me, but I'm pretty sure he was the first person ever to phone me up and ask me to write something for him, when he was the literary editor of a now-defunct newspaper in London. That doesn't mean I owe him anything, and it certainly doesn't mean I have to be nice about his book. He gave me something like one hundred and fifty quid for a thousand-word piece, so he probably still owes me. In England, writers are never nice about their friends' books: I read out a terrific sentence from *Blockbuster* with the express purpose of making a mutual friend groan with horrified envy, and it worked a treat.

With a heavy heart, then, I must tell you that *Blockbuster* is compelling, witty, authoritative, and very, very smart. Subtitled *How Hollywood Learned to Stop Worrying and Love the Summer,* it's an alternative view of the film universe to that expounded in *Easy Riders, Raging Bulls*; where Peter Biskind believes that Spielberg and Lucas murdered movies, Shone takes the view that they breathed a whole new life into them. "It seems worth pointing out: the art of popular cinema was about to get, at a rough estimate, a bazillion times better." He's not philistine about it—he

114

doesn't think that blockbusters have gotten better and better with each successive summer, for example, and he despairs in all the right places.

Indeed, he manages to put his finger on something that had always troubled my populist soul: he explains why breaking all box-office records has become a meaningless feat, almost certainly indicative of lack of quality rather than the opposite, over the last few years. *Raiders of the Lost Ark* took $8 million in its opening weekend, but then went on to make $209 million. By contrast, the big movies of 2001—*AI, Jurassic Park III, Pearl Harbor, The Mummy Returns, Planet of the Apes*—all opened big, and then disappeared fast. "By the time we've all seen that it sucked, it's a hit. The dollar value of our bum on seat has never been greater, but what it signifies has never meant less."

There is, in the end, something untrustworthy about the film critics who have sat in an audience spellbound by *Close Encounters of the Third Kind* and then gone on to slag it off at some stage in their careers. There's certainly something untrustworthy about them as critics, and I would argue that there is something untrustworthy about them as people: what was it that prevented them from responding in the way we all responded, those of us who were old enough to go to a cinema in 1977? What bit of them is missing? *Star Wars, Raiders, ET, Close Encounters,* and the rest clearly worked for discriminating cinema audiences; Tom Shone demonstrates that all his bits are where they should be by writing with acuity and enthusiasm about how and why they worked. This may be a strange thing to say about a book that embraces the evil Hollywood empire so warmly, but *Blockbuster* is weirdly humane: it prizes entertainment over boredom, and audiences over critics, and yet it's a work of great critical intelligence. It wouldn't kill me, I suppose, to say I'm proud of the boy.

I know Chris Coake, too. I taught him for a week a couple of years ago—by which I mean that I read a couple of his stories, scratched my head while trying to think of some way they could be improved, gave up the unequal struggle, and told him they were terrific. I would like to claim that I discovered him, but you can't really discover writers like this: the quality of the work is so blindingly obvious that he was never going to labor in obscurity for any length of time, and the manuscript he sent me has already been bought by Harcourt Brace in the United States, Penguin in the U.K., Guanda in Italy, and so on. You won't be able to read his book until next year, but when you see the reviews, you'll be reminded that you heard about it here first—which is, after all, how you usually hear about most things, apart from sports results.

We're in Trouble is, for the most part, a book about death—quite often, about how death affects the young. "In the Event" takes place over the course of a few hours: it begins in the early morning, just after a car crash that has killed the parents of a three-year-old boy, and ends shortly before the boy wakes up to face his terrible new world. In between times, the child's youthful and untogether godfather, who will raise the child, has a very long and very dark night of the soul. In the collection's title story, death casts a shadow over three relationships, at various stages of maturity, and with increasing directness. Sometimes, when you're reading the stories, you forget to breathe, which probably means that you read them with more speed than the writer intended. Are they literary? They're beautifully written, and they have bottom, but they're never dull, and they all contain striking and dramatic narrative ideas. And Coake never draws attention to his own art and language; he wants you to look at his people, not listen to his voice. So they're literary in the sense that they're serious, and will probably be nominated for prizes, but they're unliterary in the sense that they could end up mattering to people.

Patrick Hamilton, who died in 1962, is my new best friend. I read his most famous book, *Hangover Square,* a couple of months back; now a trilogy of novels, collectively entitled *Twenty*

Thousand Streets Under the Sky, has just been republished here in the U.K., and the first of them, *The Midnight Bell,* seemed to me to be every bit as good as *Hangover Square.* Usually, books have gone out of print for a reason, and that reason is they're no good, or, at least, of very marginal interest. (Yeah, yeah, your favorite book of all time is currently out of print, and it's a scandal. But I'll bet you any money you like it's not as good as *The Catcher in the Rye,* or *The Power and the Glory,* or anything else still available that was written in the same year.) Hamilton's books aren't arcane, or difficult, although they're dated in the sense that the culture that produced them has changed beyond recognition. Tonally, though, they're surprisingly modern: they're gritty, real, tough, and sardonic, and they deal with dissipation. And we love a bit of dissipation, don't we? We're always reading books about that. Or at least, someone's always writing one. Hamilton's version, admittedly, isn't very glamorous—people sit in pubs and get pissed. But if you were looking to fly from Dickens to Martin Amis with just one overnight stop, then Hamilton is your man. Or your airport, or whatever.

Doris Lessing called him "a marvellous novelist who's grossly neglected," and she felt that he suffered through not belonging to the 1930s Isherwood clique. She also thought, in 1968, that "his novels are true now. You can go into any pub and see it going on." This, however, is certainly no longer the case—our pub culture here in London is dying. Pubs aren't pubs anymore—not, at least, in the metropolitan center. They're discos, or sports bars, or gastro-pubs, and the working- and lower-middle-class men that Hamilton writes about with such appalled and amused fascination don't go anywhere near them. That needn't bother you, however. You're all smart enough to see that the author's central theme—men are vile and stupid, women are vile and manipulative—is as meaningful today as it ever was. I have only just started to read Nigel Jones's biography, but I suspect that Hamilton wasn't the happiest of chaps.

Thank you, dear reader, for your time over these last twelve months, if you have given any. And if you haven't, then thank you for not complaining in large enough numbers to get me slung out. I reckon I've read at least a dozen wonderful books since I began this column. I've read *Hangover Square, How to Breathe Underwater, David Copperfield, The Fortress of Solitude, George and Sam, True Notebooks, Random Family,* Ian Hamilton's Lowell biography, *The Sirens of Titan, Mystic River, Clockers, Moneyball...* And there'll be the same number this coming year, too. More, if I read faster. What have you done twelve times over the last year that was so great, apart from reading books? Fibber. ✶

OCTOBER 2004

Sex with cousins: are you for or against? I only ask because the first two books I read this month, Maile Meloy's *Liars and Saints* and Meg Rosoff's *How I Live Now,* answer the question with a resounding affirmative. (It's a long story, but in *Liars and Saints,* the couple in question is under the impression that they're actually uncle and niece, rather than cousins—and even that doesn't stop 'em! Crikey!) People are always plighting their troth to and/or screwing their cousins in Hardy and Austen, but I'd always presumed that this was because of no watercoolers, or speed-dating, or college dances; what is so dispiriting about *Liars and Saints* and *How I Live Now* is that they are set in the present, or even in the near-future, in the case of the latter book. No offense to my cousins—or, indeed, to *Believer* readers who prefer to keep things in the family—but is that really all we have to look forward to?

I know that when it comes to subconscious sexual deviation there's no such thing as coincidence, but I swear I haven't been scouring the bookshops for novels about the acceptable face of incest. I picked up *Liars and Saints* because it's been blurbed by both Helen Fielding and Philip Roth, and though I enjoyed the book, that conjunction set up an expectation that couldn't ever be fulfilled: sometimes blurbs can be too successful. I was hoping for something bubbly and yet achingly world-weary, something diverting and yet full of lacerating and unforgettable insights about the human condition, something that was fun while being at the same time no fun at all, in a bracing sort of a way, something that cheered me up while making me want to hang myself. In short, I wanted Roth and Fielding to have cowritten the book, and poor Maile Meloy couldn't deliver. *Liars and Saints* is a fresh, sweet-natured first novel, but it's no Nathan Zuckerman's *Diary*. (Cigarettes—23, attacks of *Weltschmerz*—141, etc.)

How I Live Now has had amazing reviews here in England—someone moderately sensible called it "a classic"—and although that might sometimes be enough to persuade me to shell out (cf. *Seven Types of Ambiguity*, which has received similar press), normally that wouldn't be enough to persuade me to read the thing. Rosoff's book, however, is delightfully short, and aimed at teenagers, and the publishers sent me a copy, so you can see the thinking here: knock off a classic in a day or so, at no personal expense, and bulk this column out a little. And that's pretty much how things worked out.

I'm not sure that *How I Live Now* is a classic, though, even if a book can achieve that kind of status in the month of its publication. It's set in a war-torn England a few years from now, and though the love affair between the cousins has a dreamy intensity, and Rosoff's teenage voice is strong and true, her war is a little shoddy, if you ask me. London has been occupied, but by whom no one, not even the adults, seems quite sure: it could be the French, it could be the Chinese. What sort of war is that? Rosoff is aiming for a fog of half-truth and rumor, the sort of fog that most teenagers live in most of the time, and yet one is given the impression that not even Seymour Hersh would be able to shed much light on the matter of who invaded Britain and why.

I've been meaning to read Edmund Gosse's *Father and Son* for about ten years; the only thing that was stopping me from reading it was the suspicion that it might be unreadable—miserable and dreary and impossibly remote. First published (anonymously) in 1907, *Father and Son* describes Edmund's relationship with his father, Philip, a marine biologist of some distinction who was also a member of the Plymouth Brethren, and whose fierce, joyless evangelism crippled his son's childhood. In fact, *Father and Son* is a sort of Victorian *This Boy's Life*: it's inevitably, unavoidably painful, but it's also tender and wry. OK, sometimes it reads like that Monty Python sketch about the Yorkshiremen, constantly trying to trump each other's stories of deprivation ("You lived in a hole in the road? You were lucky."): when Gosse's mother was dying of cancer, and too sick to travel from one London borough to another for the hopeless last-chance quack treatment she was trying, she and her young son stayed in a grim boarding house in Pimlico, where Edmund was allowed to entertain her by reading from religious tracts. His pathetic treat, at the end of the day, was to read her a hymn—in the Gosse family, that was what passed for fun.

My first book, *Fever Pitch,* was a memoir, and I own a copy of *Father and Son* because some clever-dick reviewer somewhere compared the two. (I seem to remember that the comparison did me no favors, before you accuse me of showing off. Someone must have been dissed, and I can't imagine it was Gosse.) My young life was blighted by my devotion to Arsenal Football Club, a team so dour and joyless during the late sixties and seventies that they would have been rather intimidated by the comparative exuberance and joie de vivre of the Plymouth Brethren. It's always weird, though, for a writer to spot the same impulses and ambitions in another, especially when the two are separated by history, culture, environment, belief, and just about anything else you can think of, and I identified absolutely with more or less every page in Gosse's book. I had hoped, when I wrote mine, that even if I were to allow myself the indulgence of writing in detail about 1960s League Cup finals, people might be prepared to put up with it if they thought there was something else going on as well; Gosse's football-sized hole was created by religion, and filled by marine biology, so he was, in effect, both damaged and repaired by his father's twin obsessions. (His father, meanwhile, was almost split in two by them—Darwin's theories were more devastating for the evangelical naturalist than for just about anyone else in the country.) *Father and Son* is an acknowledged classic, so I had expected it to be good, but I hadn't expected it to be lovable, or modern, nor had I expected it to speak to me. *How I Live Now,* by contrast, felt as if it was talking to everyone else but me—I was watching from the wings as its author addressed the multitudes. Maybe that's why you have to give books time to live before you decide that they're never going to die. You have to wait and see whether anyone in that multitude is really listening.

Every time I read a biography of a novelist, I discover that the novels in question are autobiographical to an almost horrifying degree. In Blake Bailey's book about Richard Yates, for example, we learn that Yates fictionalized his mother by changing her name from Dookie to Pookie (or perhaps from Pookie to Dookie, I can't remember now). In Nigel Jones's *Through a Glass Darkly* we learn that, like Bob in *The Midnight Bell,* Patrick Hamilton had a disastrous crush on a prostitute, and that, like Bone in *Hangover Square,* his obsession with a young actress (Geraldine Fitzgerald, who appeared in *Wuthering Heights* alongside Laurence Olivier and Merle Oberon) was deranged, although he stopped short of murdering her. And, of course, like all of his characters, Hamilton was a drunk. I'm sure that a biography of Tolkien would reveal that *The Lord of the Rings* was autobiographical, too—that Tolkien actually fell down a hole and found a place called Central Earth, where there were a whole bunch of Bobbits. Some people—critics, mostly—would argue that this diminishes the achievement somehow, but it's the writing that's hard, not the invention.

See, some of us just don't come from the right kind of background to be the subject of a literary biography. Hamilton's father was left a hundred thousand pounds in 1884, and pissed it all away during a lifetime of utter indolence and dissolution; his first wife was a prostitute whom Hamilton Sr. imagined he could save from the streets, but the marriage didn't work out. 'Snot fair! Why didn't my dad ever have a thing with prostitutes? (Note to *Believer* fact-checker: I'll give you his number, but I'm not making the call. He's pretty grouchy at the best of times.)

Jenny, the prostitute in *The Midnight Bell,* takes center stage in *The Siege of Pleasure,* the second novel in the *Twenty Thousand Streets Under the Sky* trilogy. Hamilton was a Marxist for much of his life, and though he ended up voting conservative, as so many English Marxists did, in his case it was because the Tories hated the Labor Party as much as he did, which at least shows a warped kind of ideological consistency. *The Siege of Pleasure* is in part a careful, convincing analysis of the economic and social pressures that forced Jenny onto the streets and out of her life below stairs. It's more fun than this sounds, because Hamilton, who wrote the play *Rope,* which Hitchcock later filmed, loves his ominous narratives. He's a sort of urban Hardy: everyone is doomed, right from the first page. Hamilton isolates Jenny's plight to an evening spent boozing with a tarty friend; she gets plastered, wakes up late in the house of a man she doesn't know, and fails to turn up at her new job, skivvying for a comically incapable trio of old people. It's sad, but Hamilton's laconic narrative voice is always a joy to read, and as a social historian, Hamilton is unbeatable. Who knew that you could get waiter service in pubs in the 1920s? And plates of biscuits? Biscuits! What sort of biscuits? Hamilton doesn't say.

In *So Many Books,* Gabriel Zaid attempts to grapple with the question that seems constantly to arise in this column, namely, Why bloody bother? Why bother reading the bastards, and why bother writing them? I'm not sure he gets a lot further than I've ever managed, but there are some great stats here: Zaid estimates, for example, that it would take us fifteen years simply to read a list of all the books ever published. ("Author and title"—he's very precise. You can, presumably, add on another seven or eight years if you want to know the names of the publishers.) I think he intends to make us despair, but I was actually rather heartened: not only can I now see that it's possible—I'd be finished some time in my early sixties—but I'm seriously tempted. A good chunk of coming across as educated, after all, is just a matter of knowing who wrote what: someone mentions Patrick Hamilton, and you nod sagely and say, *Hangover Square,* and that's usually enough. If I read the list, something might stick in the memory, because God knows that the books themselves don't.

Zaid's finest moment, however, comes in his second paragraph, when he says that "the truly cultured are capable of owning thousands of unread books without losing their composure or their desire for more."

That's me! And you, probably! That's us! "Thousands of unread books"! "Truly cultured"! Look at this month's list: Chekhov's letters, Amis's letters, Dylan Thomas's letters... What are the chances of getting through that lot? I've started on the Chekhov, but the Amis and the Dylan Thomas have been put straight into their permanent home on the shelves, rather than onto any sort of temporary pending pile. The Dylan Thomas I saw remaindered for fifteen quid (down from fifty) just after I'd read a terrific review of a new Thomas biography in the *New Yorker*, the Amis letters were a fiver. But as I was finding a home for them in the Arts and Lit non-fiction section (I personally find that for domestic purposes, the Trivial Pursuit system works better than Dewey), I suddenly had a little epiphany: all the books we own, both read and unread, are the fullest expression of self we have at our disposal. My music is me, too, of course—but as I only really like rock and roll and its mutations, huge chunks of me—my rarely examined operatic streak, for example—are unrepresented in my CD collection. And I don't have the wall space or the money for all the art I would want, and my house is a shabby mess, ruined by children… But with each passing year, and with each whimsical purchase, our libraries become more and more able to articulate who we are, whether we read the books or not. Maybe that's not worth the thirty-odd quid I blew on those collections of letters, admittedly, but it's got to be worth something, right? ✮

A *selection from*

TWENTY THOUSAND STREETS UNDER THE SKY

by **PATRICK HAMILTON**

★ ★ ★

The first to enter the Saloon Bar that night was Mr. Wall. This was a very sprightly little man, and another habitué. He had a red face, fair hair, twinkling blue eyes, a comic little moustache, and a bowler hat. He was obscurely connected with motors in Great Portland Street, and incorrigible. His incorrigibility was his charm. Indeed, he kept his company perpetually diverted. But this was not because his jokes and innuendoes were good, but because they were so terribly, terribly bad. You couldn't believe that any-one could behave so badly and awfully, and you loved to hear him exceed himself. Against all your sense of propriety you were obscurely tickled—simply because he was at it again. There was no doing anything with him.

His jokes, like all bad jokes, were mostly tomfooleries with the language. To call, for instance, "The Four Horsemen of the Apocalypse" "The Four Horsemen of the Eucalyptus" was, to him, quite tremendous in its sly and impudent irony. But he was not always as subtle as this. Having a wonderful comic suscept-ibility to words, and particularly those with as many as, or more than, four syllables in them, he could hardly let any hopeful ones go by without raillery. Thus, if in the course of conversation you happened innocently to employ the word "Vo*cab*ulary" he would instantly cry out "Oh my word—let's take a Cab!" or something like that, and repeat it until you had fully registered it. Or if you said that something was Identical with something else, he would say that So long as there wasn't a Dent in it, we would be all right. Or if you said that things looked rather Ominous, he would declare that So long as we weren't all run over by an Omnibus we would be all right. Or if you were so priggishly erudite as to allude to Metaphysics, he would first of all ask you, in a complaining tone, Met What?—and then add consolingly that So long as we Met it Half Way it would be all right. It was a kind of patter in the conditional. Similarly, in his own particular idiom, Martyrs were associated with Tomatoes, Waiters with Hot Potatoes, Cribbage with Cabbage, Salary with Celery (the entire vegetable world was ineffably droll), Suits with Suet, Fiascoes with Fiancées, and the popular wireless genius with Macaroni. He was, perhaps, practically off his head.

"Well, Bob, my boy," he said, rallying, as he came in. "How're you? B an' B, please, calgirl."

He employed the popular abbreviation for Bitter and Button mixed, and Ella gave it him, primly and deprecatingly, and took his money.

"How're you, Mr. Wall?" she said. "We haven't seen you lately."

"Oh, I'm all right. Wotyavin, Bob?"

"I won't have nothing to-night, thank you, Mr. Wall."

"What—You on the Wagon?"

"Pro Tem," said Bob.

" 'Bout time he was," said Ella.

At this the door creaked open, and Mr. Sounder entered.

"Ah ha!" said Mr. Sounder. "The worthy Mr. Wall!"

"Oh ho!" said Mr. Wall. "The good Mr. Sounder!" But the two gentlemen looked at each other with a kind of glassy gleam which belied this broad and amicable opening. Indeed, these two were notoriously incapable of hitting it off, and the thwarted condescension of the one, together with the invulnerable impudence of the other, were features of "The Midnight Bell" in the evening.

"Been writin' any more letters to those papers of yours, Mr. Sounder?" asked Mr. Wall.

"Not my papers—alas—Mr. Wall. Bitter I think, please, Ella."

"Wish I owned a paper, 'tanyrate," said Ella, trying to keep the peace, and she gave him his beer.

"No…" said Mr. Sounder. "As a matter of Absolute Fact, within the last hour I have been in the Throes of Composition."

"So long as it ain't a *false* position," said Mr. Wall. "It's all right."

Here both Bob and Ella were seized by that irritating and inexplicable desire to giggle, and showed it on their shamefaced faces: but Mr. Sounder ignored the interruption.

"I have, in fact, brought forth a Sonnet," he said.

"A Sonnet?" said Bob.

"Oh," said Mr. Wall. "Didn't know you wore a Bonnet. Glad to hear it."

"What's the subject?" asked Bob.

("You might lend it to me," said Mr. Wall.)

"The subject is Evensong in Westminster Abbey," said Mr. Sounder, suavely, and looked portentously at his beer. ✶

NOVEMBER 2004

I have been meaning to read a book about cricket for awhile, with the sole intention of annoying you all. I even toyed with the idea of reading only cricket books this entire month, but then I realized that this would make it too easy for you to skip the whole column; this way, you have to wade through the cricket to get to the Chekhov and the Roddy Doyle. I'm presuming here that very few of you have ever seen a cricket match, and if you have, you are almost certain to have been both mystified and stupefied: this, after all, is a game that, in its purest form (there are all sorts of cheap-thrills bastardized versions now), lasts for five days and very frequently ends in a tie: five days is not quite long enough to get through everything that needs doing in a cricket match, especially as you can't play in the rain.

The funny thing is that we actually do like cricket here in England—it's not some hey-nonny-no phony heritage thing, like Morris dancing (horrific bearded men with sticks and bells) or cream teas. Thirty or forty years ago it was our equivalent of base-ball, an all-consuming summer sport that drove football off the back pages of newspapers completely for three months; now Beckham and the rest of them get the headlines even when they're lying on Caribbean beaches. But big international matches still sell out, and every now and again the England team starts winning, and we renew our interest.

Ed Smith reminds traditionalists of a time when cricketers were divided into two camps, "Gentlemen" and "Players"; the for-mer were private-school boys and university graduates from upper-middle-class backgrounds, the latter horny-handed profes-sionals who weren't even allowed to share a dressing room with their social betters. Smith is a Cambridge graduate who reviews fiction for one of the broadsheet newspapers. He's also good-looking, well-spoken, articulate, and he has played for England, so perhaps not surprisingly, *On and Off the Field,* his diary of a season, attracted a fair bit of attention, all of it, as far as I can tell, admir-ing. Where's the fairness in that? You'd think that if critics had any use at all, it would be to give our golden boys and girls a fearsome bashing, but of course you can't even rely on them for that.

To be fair to the critics, Smith didn't give them much ammu-nition: *On and Off the Field* is terrific, exactly the sort of book you want from a professional sportsman but you never get: it's self-ana-lytical (even if, after the self-analysis, he attributes some of his early-season failure to sheer bad luck), wry, and honest. The sports memoir is such a debased form—George Best, the biggest football star of the sixties and seventies, has "written" five autobiographies to date, and he hasn't kicked a ball for thirty-odd years—but *On and Off the Field* is different: the photo on the back depicts Smith slumped against a wall, the very epitome of defeated misery. Defeated misery is what all sport is about, eventually, if you follow the story for long enough; all sportsmen know this, but Smith is one of the very few capable not only of recognizing this bitter truth, but acknowledging it in print. I know you're not going to read it. But let's say I've read it on your behalf, and we've all enjoyed it.

To my surprise, I managed to read, in its entirety, one of the many books of collected letters I inexplicably bought last month. Why I read it, however, is almost as mysterious as why I bought it in the first place; or rather, I'm not sure why I felt I had to read every word of every letter. After a little while, you get the pattern: letters to his feckless brothers tend to be fiercely admonitory (and therefore fun); letters to his mother and sister tend to be purely domestic, functional, and a little on the dull side ("Tell Arseny to water the birch tree once a week, and the eucalyptus"); letters to his wife, Olga Knipper, are embarrassingly slushy, and the letters he wrote to Alexey Suvorin, his publisher, are the letters I was hoping for when I started the book: they're the ones where you're most likely to find something about writing. I should have stuck to the Suvorin letters, but you get addicted to the (mostly sleepy) rhythms of Chekhov's quotidian life.

Chekhov, as you probably know (I don't know why, but I always think of you lot knowing everything, pretty much, apart from the rules of cricket), started life as a hack, a journalist who wrote short comic articles for various Russian periodicals while training and then practicing as a doctor. And then, in 1886, when he was just beginning to take his writing more seriously, he received the sort of letter most young writers can only dream of getting. Dmitry Grigorovich, a respected older novelist, wrote out of the blue to tell him he was a genius, and he should stop pissing around.

I know from personal experience that these letters have a galvanizing effect at first. But once you've had twenty or thirty of them, you start to chuck them straight into the bin once you've checked out the signature. I had a rule that I'd only take any notice if the correspondent had a Pulitzer or a Nobel; if you get involved with every two-bit literary legend who wants to be your friend, you'd never get any work done. Some of them can be a real pain. (Salinger? Reclusive? Yeah, I wish.) Anyway, Chekhov's reply to Grigorovich is every bit as humbled, as sweetly thunderstruck, as you'd want it to be.

"Everyone has seen a *Cherry Orchard* or an *Uncle Vanya,* while very few have even heard of 'The Wife' or 'In the Ravine,'" says Janet Malcolm in her short, moving, clever book *Reading Chekhov.* Perhaps this isn't the right time to talk about what "everyone" means here, although one is entitled to stop and wonder at the world in which our men and women of letters live—not "everyone" has seen a football match or an episode of *Seinfeld,* let alone a nineteenth-century Russian play. But she's right, of course, to point out that his stories languish in relative obscurity. In his introduction to the *Essential Tales,* Richard Ford writes about tackling the stories before he was old enough to realize that their plainness was deceptive, and though I hate that "writers' writer" stuff (after a lifetime of reading, I can officially confirm that readers' writers beat writers' writers every time), I can see what he means. When you're young and pretentious, you want your Greats to come with bells on, otherwise you can't see what the fuss is about, and there are no bells in those stories.

What's remarkable about the letters is that the drama hardly comes up at all. Every now and again, Chekhov tells someone that he's just written a rubbish new play, or that he's hopeless at the craft. "Reading through my newly born play convinces me more than ever that I'm not a playwright," he says when writing to Suvorin about *The Seagull; Three Sisters* is "boring, sluggish and awkward." He'd have been staggered at the way things have turned out. His working life was about prose—and money. He tells just about anyone who'll listen how much he got for this, and how much they could get for that.

The letters are full of useful advice—advice that holds good even now. "Sleeping with a whore, breathing right in her mouth, endlessly listening to her pissing... where's the sense in that? Civilized people don't simply obey their baser instincts. They demand more from a woman than bed, horse sweat and the sound of pissing." He's right, of course. There's no sense in that, at all. But that pissing sound is sort of addictive after a few years, isn't it? If you haven't even started listening to it, then I can only urge you never to do so.

Apart from the peculiar obsession with the sound of pissing, there's a modern writing life described here. There's the money thing, of course, but there's also gossip, and endless charitable activity, and fame. (Chekhov was recognized everywhere he went.) He's also the only genius I've come across who had no recognition of, or interest in, the immensity of his own talent.

As a special bonus, you also get some of those bad biopic comedy moments thrown in. "I went to see Lev Tolstoy the day before yesterday," he writes to Gorky. "He was full of praise for you, and said you were a 'splendid writer.' He likes your 'The Fair' and 'In The Steppe,' but not 'Malva.'" You just know that there's only three words in this letter Gorky would have registered, and that he spent the rest of the day too depressed to get out of bed.

This month, my bookshelves functioned exactly as they are supposed to. I'd just finished the Chekhov and dimly remembered buying Janet Malcom's book when it was first published. And then I found it, and read it. And enjoyed it. You forget that the very best literary critics are capable of being very clever about people and life, as well as books: there's a brilliant passage here where Malcolm, who is travelling around Russia visiting Chekhov's houses, links her feelings over the return of a lost bag to her feelings about travel:

"[Our homes] are where the action is; they are where the riches of experience are distributed... Only when faced with one of the inevitable minor hardships of travel do we break out of the trance of tourism and once again feel the sharp savor of the real." I can't understand, though, why she thinks that the letters between Chekhov and Olga Knipper "make wonderful reading." I've only read Chekhov's side, but she seems to have reduced the man to mush: "My little doggie," "my dear little dog," "my darling doggie," "Oh, doggie, doggie," "my little dog," "little ginger-haired doggie," "my coltish little doggie," "my lovely little mongrel doggie," "my darling, my perch," "my squiggly one," "dearest little colt," "my incomparable little horse," "my dearest chaffinch"... For god's sake, pull yourself together, man! You're a major cultural figure!

Knipper and Chekhov were together only rarely in their short marriage (she was acting in St. Petersburg, he was trying to keep warm in Yalta) and Malcolm seems to suggest rather sadly that famous men and women with more conventional relationships rob biographers of future source material, because they have no reason to write to each other. On the evidence here, all couples should be compelled by law to spend twenty-four hours a day together, three hundred and sixty-five days a year, just in case either partner is tempted to call the other a chaffinch, or a perch, or an aardvark, in writing.

Malcolm, however, is one of those people so sweetly devoted to her subject that she won't recognize flaws as flaws, but as strengths—or, at least, as *characteristics*. There's this pedestal—I don't know anyone who's even seen it, but it's there—and once you're up on it, people stop telling you that you can't do this, or you're useless at that, and start wondering why you have allowed something that *looks* like uselessness to appear in your work. Christopher Ricks did it in his recent book *Dylan's Visions of Sin*: he becomes very troubled by a ropy rhyme ("rob them"/"problem") in "Positively Fourth Street," and then nags at it until the ropy rhyme becomes yet another example of Bob's genius: "It must be granted that if these lines induce queasiness, they do make a point of saying 'No, I do not feel that good.' So an unsettling rhyme such as *problem/rob them* might rightly be hard to stomach…" The notion that Dylan might have just thought, "Oh, fuck it, that'll do" never crosses Ricks's mind for a moment.

Malcolm does her own, perhaps more self-aware version of this when talking about the troublingly "abrupt" and "unmotivated" changes of character in Chekhov's stories: "after enough time goes by, a great writer's innovations stop looking like mistakes." See, I'm still at that early stage, where everything still looks like a mistake, so I would have liked Ms. Malcolm to be a little more precise with the figures here. What's "enough time"? Just, you know, roughly? Are we talking six months? Two years? I don't really want to have to wait much longer than that.

I've known Roddy Doyle for a while now. I read him before I met him, and the Barrytown trilogy was an important source of inspiration for me when I was starting out: who knew that books written with such warmth and simplicity could be so complex and intelligent? On this side of the Atlantic, at least, Doyle single-handedly redefined what we mean by "literary" fiction. *Oh, Play That Thing* is the second part of the trilogy that began with *A Star Called Henry*; it's set in the United States during the twenties and thirties, and features Louis Armstrong as a central character, so I've been reading it while listening to *Hot Fives and Sevens* on my iPod.

Reading reviews and interviews with him over the last few weeks, one is reminded that there's nothing critics like less than a writer producing something that he hasn't done before—apart, that is, from a writer producing more of the same. One reviewer complained that Doyle used to write short books, and now they've gone fat; another that he used to write books set in Dublin, and he should have kept them there; another that he used to write with a child's-eye view, and now he's writing about adults.

All of these criticisms, of course, could have been based on the catalog copy, rather than on the book itself—a two-line synopsis and information about the number of pages would have received exactly the same treatment. You're half-expecting someone to point out that back in the day he used to write books that sold for a tenner, and now they've gone up to seventeen quid.

What he's doing, of course, is the only thing a writer can do: he's writing the books that he wants, in the way he wants to. He wants to write about different things, and to add something to the natural talent that produced those early books. I wouldn't want to read anyone who did anything else—apart from P. G. Wodehouse, who did exactly the same thing hundreds of times over. So where does that leave us? Pretty much back where we started, I suppose. That's the beauty of this column, even if I do say it myself. ✶

A selection from

A LIFE IN LETTERS
by ANTON CHEKHOV

★ ★ ★

Y ou have only one fault. But in that fault lies the falseness of
your position, your discontent and even the catarrh in your
bowels. It is your complete lack of manners. Please forgive me, but
veritas magis amicitiae... The fact of the matter is that there are certain rules in life... You will always feel uncomfortable among
intelligent people, out of place and inadequate, unless you are
equipped with the manners to cope... Your talent has opened the
door for you into this milieu, you should be perfectly at home in
it, but at the same time something pulls you away from it and you
find yourself having to perform a kind of balancing act between
these cultivated circles on the one hand and the people you live
among on the other. That telltale lower-class flesh of yours is all
too apparent, the result of growing up with the rod, next to the
wine cellar, and subsisting on handouts. It is hard to rise above
that, terribly hard!

Civilized people must, I believe, satisfy the following criteria:

1) They respect human beings as individuals and are therefore
always tolerant, gentle, courteous and amenable... They do
not create scenes over a hammer or a mislaid eraser; they do
not make you feel they are conferring some great benefit on
you when they live with you, and they don't make a scandal
when they leave, saying "it's impossible to live with you!"
They put up with noise and cold, over-done meat, jokes, and
the presence of strangers in the house...

2) They have compassion for other people besides beggars

137

and cats. Their hearts suffer the pain of what is hidden to the naked eye. So for example, if Pyotr realized that his father and mother are turning grey from worry and depression and are lying awake at nights because they see him so seldom (and when they do, he's the worse for drink), he hastens to see them and cuts out the vodka. Civilized people lie awake worrying about how to help the Polevayevs, to pay for their brothers to go through University, to see their mother decently clothed...

3) They respect other people's property, and therefore pay their debts.

4) They are not devious, and they fear lies as they fear fire. They don't tell lies even in the most trivial matters. To lie to someone is to insult them, and the liar is diminished in the eyes of the person he lies to. Civilized people don't put on airs; they behave in the street as they would do at home, they don't show off to impress their juniors... They are discreet and don't broadcast unsolicited confidences... They mostly keep silence, from respect for others' ears.

5) They don't run themselves down in order to provoke the sympathy of others. They don't play on other people's heart-strings to be sighed over and cosseted. They don't say: "No one understands me!" or "I've wasted my talents on trivial doodlings! I'm a whore!!" because all that sort of thing is just cheap striving for effects, it's vulgar, old hat and false...

6) They are not vain. They don't waste time with the fake jewellery of hobnobbing with celebrities, being permitted to shake the hand of a drunken Plevako, the exaggerated bon-homie of the first person they meet at the Salon, being the

life and soul of the bar... They regard phrases like "I am a representative of the Press!!"—the sort of thing one only hears from people like Rozdevich and Levenberg—as absurd. If they have done a brass farthing's work they don't pass it off as if it were 100 roubles' by swanking about with their portfolios, and they don't boast of being able to gain admission to places other people aren't allowed in... True talent always sits in the shade, mingles with the crowd, avoids the limelight... As Krylov said, the empty barrel makes more noise than the full one...

7) If they do possess talent, they value it. They will sacrifice people of mind, women, wine, and the bustle and vanity of the world for it... They take pride in it. So they don't go boozing with school teachers or with people who happen to have come to stay with Skvortsov; they know they have a responsibility to exert a civilizing influence on them rather than aimlessly hanging out with them. And they are fastidious in their habits...

8) They work at developing their aesthetic sensibility. They do not allow themselves to sleep in their clothes, stare at the bedbugs in the cracks in the walls, breathe foul air, walk on a floor covered in spit, cook their food on a paraffin stove. As far as possible they try to control and elevate their sex drive... Sleeping with a whore, breathing right in her mouth, endlessly listening to her pissing, putting up with her stupidity and never moving a step away from her—where's the sense in that? Civilized people don't simply obey their baser instincts. They demand more from a woman than bed, horse sweat and the sound of pissing and more in the way of intelligence than an ability to swell up with a phantom pregnancy; artists above all need freshness, refinement, humanity, the capacity to be a

mother, not just a hole... They don't continually swill vodka, they're aware they're not pigs so they don't root about sniffing in cupboards. They drink when they want to, as free men... For they require *mens sana in corpore sano*.

And so on. That's what civilized people are like... Reading *Pickwick* and learning a speech from *Faust* by heart is not enough if your aim is to become a truly civilized person and not to sink below the level of your surroundings. Taking a cab over to Yakimanka and then decamping a week later is not enough...

What you must do is work unceasingly, day and night, read constantly, study, exercise willpower... Every hour is precious...

Shuttling backwards and forwards to Yakimanka won't help. You must roll up your sleeves and make a clean break, once and for all... Come back to us, smash the vodka bottle and settle down to read... even if it's just Turgenev whom you've never read...

You've got to get over your fucking vanity, you're not a child any more... you'll soon be thirty! Time to grow up!

I'm expecting you... We all are...

Your

A. Chekhov *

INDEX OF STUFF HE'S BEEN READING

The author wishes to thank the following for their help: Andrew Leland, Gideon Lewis-Kraus, Eli Horowitz, Chris Gage, Sam Potts, Zelda Turner, Rachel Cugnoni, Dave and Serge, Charlotte Moore, Tony Hoagland, David Downs, Mac Barnett, Claire Caleshu, Shannon DeJong, Jordan Bass, Soo Oh, Brian Rogers, Howard Wyman, and Rachel Swaby.

Grateful acknowledgement is made to the following for permission to reprint previously published material: A selection from Charlotte Moore's *George and Sam: Autism in the Family* appears courtesy of Viking Penguin UK, 2004. Tony Hoagland's "Impossible Dream" from *What Narcissism Means to Me*, published by Graywolf Press, is reprinted here courtesy of the author. A selection from *Twenty Thousand Streets Under the Sky* appears courtesy of the estate of Patrick Hamilton. A selection from from Anton Chekhov's *A Life in Letters*, translated by Rosamund Bartlett and Anthony Phillips, is reprinted here courtesy of Penguin UK.

Half of the proceeds from this book will go to:

TREEHOUSE

T he TreeHouse Trust is a U.K. charity based in central London, established in 1997 to provide an educational Centre of Excellence for children with autism.

TreeHouse was set up by a North London group of parents of children recently diagnosed with autism. Despite the fact that research supported the crucial importance of early, intensive education for children with autism, there was nothing available for their children, nor for the thousands of similar children they wish to help. In just five years, TreeHouse has attracted widespread national and international recognition for its pioneering achievements from the medical and educational establishment.

From an initial pupil base of four, the school now has forty pupils and aims to accommodate eighty pupils within the next ten years. Further, TreeHouse needs to extend its help to the tens of thousands of other children with autism in the U.K. TreeHouse is developing plans to disseminate its teaching model and to secure the funds for a permanent building from which TreeHouse can grow the school and offer national facilities for training and education research.

FOR MORE INFORMATION OR TO MAKE A DONATION:
VISIT: www.treehouse.org.uk
EMAIL: info@treehouse.org.uk
CALL: 0044 208 815 5433
OR WRITE TO: TreeHouse, Woodside Avenue, London, N10 3JA

The other half of the proceeds from this book will go to:

826NYC

826NYC is a nonprofit organization dedicated to supporting students ages six to eighteen with their creative and expository writing skills, and to helping teachers inspire their students to write. Our services are structured around our belief that great leaps in learning can happen with one-on-one attention and that strong writing skills are fundamental to future success.

Our writing center shares a space with the Brooklyn Superhero Supply Co., a retail store that helps raise funds for the center's writing programs and engages students' enthusiasm and interest. Students and volunteers slip through a revolving bookcase to enter the writing center, where we offer writing workshops, publishing projects, and one-on-one help with homework and English language learning. All of our programs are challenging and enjoyable, and ultimately strengthen each student's power to express ideas effectively, creatively, confidently, and in his or her individual voice.

FOR MORE INFORMATION OR TO MAKE A DONATION:
VISIT: www.826nyc.org
EMAIL: info@826nyc.org
CALL: 718.499.9884
OR WRITE TO: 372 Fifth Avenue, Brooklyn, NY 11215

Nick Hornby is the author of five previous books. His next, a novel entitled *A Long Way Down*, will be published by Riverhead in May 2005. He lives in Highbury, north London, with his partner Amanda and his three sons.

NICK HORNBY WILL NOT STOP READING

AND NEITHER SHOULD YOU!

In addition to Nick Hornby's monthly column, every issue of the *Believer* features terrific essays from writers like Rick Moody, Paul Collins, and Michelle Tea, along with interviews with the likes of David Foster Wallace, George Saunders, Janet Malcolm, Shirley Hazzard, Ice Cube, Shirin Neshat, and Ashida Kim (who is a ninja). Maureen Howard called the *Believer* "a wealth of intelligence, energy, and wit." Don't miss a single issue!

visit us online at
www.believermag.com
and fill out the below form for a special discount!